MOMBASA

MOMBASA

An African City

Harm J. de Blij

NORTHWESTERN UNIVERSITY PRESS 1968

The research for this volume and its publication were supported
by the Michigan State University African Studies Center

Library of Congress catalog card number: 68–17731

Manufactured in the United States of America

Harm J. de Blij is Professor of Geography and Associate Director of
the African Studies Center at Michigan State University.

111087

CONTENTS

LIST OF MAPS

PREFACE

THIS IS THE THIRD of a series of studies dealing with the form and structure of African cities. The first, an article focusing upon Lourenço Marques, Moçambique, was published in 1962. The second, a monograph on Dar es Salaam, Tanzania, appeared in 1963. The field work out of which the present volume emerged was begun in 1962, continued in 1963, and completed in 1966. It was made possible through a grant from the African Studies Center, Office of International Programs, of Michigan State University. The cartography and photography, as well as the preparation of several drafts, were facilitated by All-University Grants awarded regularly to Michigan State University faculty engaged in research activities. I wish to express my appreciation for this assistance and especially for the support of Dr. Charles C. Hughes, Director of the African Studies Center, and Dr. Lawrence M. Sommers, Chairman of the Department of Geography, who aided me in a variety of ways.

Elsewhere I have stated the objectives of these studies; it will suffice only to repeat that the data here recorded are available to other geographers whose interests in or acquaintance with specialized research techniques may carry the inquiry in a different direction. I was gratified to note that previous work has led others to make some comparisons, and the city in newly independent Africa may change more rapidly than we at first thought.

Many persons were of material assistance in the research and writing of this volume. The initial field recording was done by Mr. A. Mascarenhas of the University College, Dar es Salaam. Three of my graduate students joined me in East Africa in 1966. Mr. Donald L. Capone assisted me in the field work leading to the map of Urban Land Use and the sketches of the mainland areas, and without his talents for field recording we would not have succeeded. Mr. S. S. Birdsall managed to secure several base maps that were out of print and did a search of all air photo coverage; additionally he located the materials filed in the Vice President's Office at Nairobi and obtained permission to inspect them. He was able to do all this while carrying on his own research in Kenya and Tanzania. Mr. A. Nazzaro did a preliminary reconnaissance and took some of the photographs. Mr. S. Ramtu provided me with a large number of contacts in Mombasa and made himself available for useful discussions.

As readers of this volume will perceive, Mombasa changed even during the course of this study. For example, street names were altered with the coming of independence, and some of our older base maps still carry Makupa Road instead of the name Jomo Kenyatta Avenue. Most of the new names, however, were used throughout the volume. Mr. Capone drew the base upon which the retail functions were recorded, and it should be emphasized that while these bases are "After Survey of Kenya" (Chapter 5), the recorded data are not. Mr. Capone also did most of the work on Map 2, but he is not responsible for any of the other cartography, which, I know he would wish me to record here, was done by the author.

Most of the oblique air photographs used in this book were provided by the Quality Photo Process Company, an establishment which has done business in Mombasa for many years and which remained true to its reputation for helpfulness. I was able to obtain precisely what was needed. Those photographs which are not acknowledged were taken by the author.

Finally, I should like to pay tribute to Mombasa, one of the most pleasant places on the continent of Africa or, for that matter, anywhere. It seemed to be impossible to stop without being offered directions by helpful people. Everyone responded willingly when questions were asked; at one time a city police officer, finding us with car trouble, led the way to the nearest service station and saved us hours of inconvenience. To us, it was a gesture that well reflected the atmosphere in this beautiful city.

HARM J. DE BLIJ

Coral Gables, Florida
February 11, 1967

MOMBASA

Chapter 1 INTRODUCTION
TO MOMBASA

ALONG FOUR THOUSAND MILES of East Africa's tropical coastline, Mombasa ranks as the largest and most important port city. Mombasa's seaport, the best equipped of East Africa's coastal terminals, serves as the sole effective outlet for landlocked Uganda and constitutes the only ocean port of Kenya. Mombasa is connected by rail and road to Nairobi and the Kenya Highlands, to Kampala and the most productive (southern) part of Uganda, and to the Moshi and Arusha Districts of northeastern Tanzania (Map 1). In 1965 Mombasa's port handled over four and a half million tons of cargo —nearly five times as large a volume as passed through Dar es

3

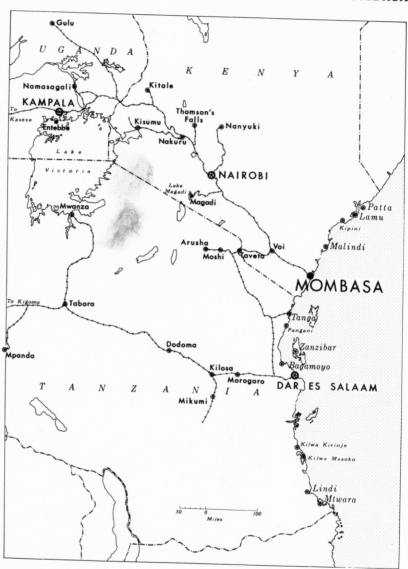

MAP 1

Salaam and putting it in a class with Lourenço Marques and Durban.[1]

Mombasa, furthermore, is one of East Africa's largest urban centers. The 1962 population was just under 180,000, and with its immediate environs the urban area counts over 200,000 inhabitants.[2] On the basis of census data, Mombasa appears to be maintaining its lead over its coastal rival: Dar es Salaam in 1962 had 150,000 residents. Mombasa, thus, is the second largest city in a vast and populous region, whose leading city, Nairobi, lies in its immediate hinterland.

Unlike Nairobi and Dar es Salaam, however, Mombasa is an old city. Many of the larger urban centers in Africa south of the Sahara (and especially south of the equator) were founded and developed by European colonial powers and carry a dominant Western imprint as a result.[3] But Mombasa was an established settlement centuries before modern European colonizers first saw the coasts of East Africa. It is believed that its site was selected by Persians, who are said to have named it after a town then existing called Mombaza, in what is today Oman. For nearly a thousand years since then, settlement here has been more or less continuous, and Mombasa eventually emerged from among its competitors as a focal point in eastern Africa for maritime trade. As such, it fell victim to the campaigns of colonial rivals, and the town was repeatedly devastated. Indeed, the Swahili name for Mombasa is *Mvita*, which, according to the most generally accepted interpretation, means "place of war." [4] The long period of unchallenged Arab domination of coastal East Africa ended when the Portuguese arrived on the

1. The volume at Dar es Salaam was 922,000 tons; at Mombasa it was 4,512,000 tons. See *Annual Report, 1965: East African Railways and Harbours*, Government Printer (Nairobi, 1966), pp. 25, 26.

2. *Kenya Population Census, 1962*, Economics and Statistics Division, Ministry of Finance and Economic Planning (Nairobi, 1964), p. 15. For data on population and related aspects see W. T. W. Morgan and N. Manfred Shaffer, *Population of Kenya* (Nairobi, 1966).

3. For a summary of some aspects of this European imprint see B. E. Thomas, "The Colonial Imprint on African Cities," *Annals of the Association of American Geographers*, LII, no. 3 (September, 1962), 71–72.

4. The derivation of the word *Mvita* is still a matter for debate. Another view is that it is related to *fita* (hidden, concealed), a descriptive term for the site of Mombasa.

scene, and as early as 1505 Mombasa fell to the new invaders. Subsequently Mombasa came under the control of the ruler of the Zanzibar Sultanate, and still later British overlordship sanctioned this merger by creating, along the coast, a Kenya Protectorate under the administration of Zanzibar. Ultimately the connection with Zanzibar was severed, and the Kenya Protectorate (a strip of mainland 10 miles wide and 52 miles in length, including the port) was formally attached to the sovereign Republic of Kenya.

Thus Mombasa for centuries has been a busy crossroads, although the port's rise to eminence among coastal East African cities has occurred quite recently. Africans, Arabs, Asians, and Europeans have become permanent residents of the town, the multiracial character of which is reflected by the contribution of each sector to the urban landscape. There are other cities in East Africa with similar population components, but Mombasa, as this study will show, in many ways is unique among them.

Through its lengthy history Mombasa had many competitors for the maritime trade of the western Indian Ocean, and during certain periods other East African ports overshadowed it. Today, however, Mombasa eclipses all of those cities which continue to function as ports—Mogadishu, Zanzibar, Moçambique Island—while Pata, Lamu, Malindi, Kilwa, Sofala, and others have lost all their former importance (Fig. 1).[5] The bases for Mombasa's prominence do not form a central concern for this study, but they consist of historical incident and accident and geographical advantage and opportunity. Mombasa's former competitors lie both to the north and to the south of the island city. Northward, the East Coast displays both cultural and physical transitions. The former is reflected, for example, by the presence of Somali residents in the town in contrast to Dar es Salaam, a mere two hundred miles to the south.[6] The latter transition involves a rapid change from savanna to steppe conditions and eventually to the deserts of the Horn. Not only does the coast

5. For details see K. Ingham, *A History of East Africa* (London, 1962). A more concise outline is given in L. W. Hollingsworth, *A Short History of the East Coast of Africa* (London, 1959).

6. For a breakdown of the African population of Mombasa District see *Kenya Population Census, 1962*, p. 60. In addition to a total of 15 Ogaden and Gurreh residents, some 267 people are accounted for as Somali-speaking.

FIGURE 1. The town of Lamu, once a competitor for Mombasa on the East African coast, is now a small settlement, totally eclipsed by its former rival. Communications with the interior are poor, and only some dhows call at the once busy port. (Quality Photo Process)

north of Mombasa become rapidly drier; inland areas show a similar decline in precipitation, as savanna gives way to scrub. East-central and northeastern Kenya are drought-stricken areas, capable only of supporting a semi-sedentary population (with the exception of the Tana River Valley).

Southward, the distance from the interior core regions rapidly depreciates the value of sites which otherwise would be potentially suitable. In addition, access to the Kenya Highlands and the lakes region, in terms of terrain and environment, is no more difficult from Mombasa than it is from other coastal locations.

THE PAST

These are modern-day advantages, however, and they are related to Mombasa's role as a break-of-bulk point between maritime trade routes and a developing hinterland. Less than a century ago Mombasa did not, for practical purposes, possess a hinterland as such; it was not connected by permanent routes to the interior for which it serves today as the major outlet. The direct influence of the town was felt perhaps a dozen miles inland, and its orientation was oceanward rather than landward, toward Zanzibar and other places on the shores of the Indian Ocean rather than toward the highland savannas and lakes of East Africa. Most of what constitutes Mombasa today was built during the past three-quarters of a century, when contact with the hinterland was achieved. Yet Mombasa was a place of activity for centuries prior to this period and could boast a settlement of permanence, large parts of which can still be observed in the urban landscape of today. Indeed, it was a place of importance, as many bitter wars for hegemony over the site can attest. Some of these struggles can be ascribed to internal rivalries among wealthy and powerful Arab families, but others were full-scale hostilities between competing colonial forces. What was so attractive about this insular coastal station?

First of all Mombasa was a strategic place. The original harbor, on the eastern side of the island, had a narrow entrance and afforded good protection. But until the Portuguese recognized the possibilities of rendering this harbor secure by constructing a fortification, Mombasa, like Malindi, Lamu, and the other coastal settlements, was but one of a string of village trading stations, and there was little or nothing to suggest that it would become a focus of activity. Indeed, Malindi, 75 miles to the north, would have appeared to possess a brighter future.

For Mombasa, the Portuguese decision to build a fortified outpost against the northern enemies was a fateful one, for it assured the settlement of the attentions of all those who, in the centuries that followed, sought power along the East African coast. Portugal had failed to secure Mombasa permanently after the 1505 capitulation of the town, and after nearly ninety years of intermittent and costly fighting, the building of Fort Jesus was begun in 1593. The fort, large parts of which still stand today overlooking the older sections of Mombasa, quickly became the prize of the East African coast (Fig. 2) and was the scene of murderous battles and sieges.

FIGURE 2. Fort Jesus as it appears from the waters of Mombasa Harbor. The first phase of construction began in 1593, when the Portuguese selected Mombasa as a stronghold. Subsequently the Europeans were ousted, and Arab flags flew over the fort, the scene of many bloody battles. (Quality Photo Process)

For Malindi, Mombasa's rival, the Portuguese selection of a new headquarters was a disaster of sorts, for the removal of the garrison meant that hundreds of traders and workers likewise sought residence at Mombasa. Even the Sultan of Malindi relocated his residence and assumed a new title, Sultan of Mombasa, adding greater significance to the place. From then on, many a struggle culminated in a contest for Fort Jesus, and many a rebellion was born in Mombasa. The Portuguese eventually lost their foothold and withdrew to Moçambique, and before the British established themselves over coastal East Africa, another period of Arab domination occurred.

THE PRESENT

Mombasa, then, for almost a thousand years developed as a part of the Indian Ocean littoral, with its Arab and Asian influences, rather than as an African settlement upon which some foreign impact can be recorded. Mombasa was a world apart in East Africa, and many a traveler described it so. But with British overlordship in this part of East Africa a wholly new phase of development began, which has seen in three generations the rise of a modern city, a city which overflows onto the mainland. The old harbor now is a port of call only for dhows and small craft, and a new, modern port has been developed on the opposite (western) side of the island.

And yet Mombasa retains an atmosphere that is quite unique in East Africa, even when compared to such places as Tanga and Dar es Salaam. Visible links remain, not only in the remnants of Fort Jesus and the fresh-water wells that served visiting ships, but in the very street pattern of the Old Town that spreads northward and westward from the fort (Fig. 3) and in the buildings and graveyards of another century (Figs. 4, 5). The dhows still ply the coasts of East Africa and Arabia, they still rely on the monsoon to complete their trading cycle, and they still bring supplies of salt and other goods to the old port, as they have for centuries. The faces in a Mombasa crowd, the goods selling on the local markets, and the religious shrines scattered through the town all are reminders that here half the world's cultures have met and come to terms, each contributing to the uniqueness of this city.

THE PURPOSE OF THIS STUDY

Is it possible to arrive at a greater understanding of the dimensions of urban development in a multiracial setting by focusing upon the spatial aspects of such urban centers? Previous studies suggest that useful insights do emerge from such efforts. From a study of Lourenço Marques it was possible to identify the imprint of a transplanted culture by means somewhat more reliable than those based rather subjectively upon building styles, sidewalk cafés, and

FIGURE 3. The Old Town (*A* on photograph) is located directly northwest of Fort Jesus (center). The site of Old Town has witnessed centuries of settlement, and its street pattern and buildings form a direct link with the distant past. (Quality Photo Process)

inlaid *trottoirs*.[7] Moçambique has not yet witnessed the transition to African rule, but this event has taken place in Dar es Salaam, capital of Tanzania. There, African control exists over an urban center which was founded by the ruler of the Arab Sultanate of Zanzibar, initially developed by German interests and subsequently taken over by British rule. Each of these successive administrations has made some impact upon the form and structure of the city, and now the African period has begun. How long will previous patterns remain evident? Which of these will prove to be most permanent? Will the racial residential segregation found to exist at the termination of colonial rule break down, and if so, permanently or temporarily? In both Lourenço Marques and Dar es Salaam, a racio-eco-

7. H. J. de Blij, "The Functional Structure and Central Business District of Lourenço Marques, Moçambique," *Economic Geography*, XXXVIII, no. 1 (January, 1962), 56–77.

FIGURE 4. A graveyard of another century, located in the Old Town in the shadow of Fort Jesus, is a silent reminder of the thousands who died in the almost endless series of struggles for hegemony over the island. (A. Nazzaro)

nomic division within the central business district emerged when specific retail functions were mapped.[8] Among the objectives of the present study is a similar dissection of the central business district of Mombasa (which will hereafter be called the CBD).

The primary objective of this study is to determine the nature of the contributions made, in the development of the site of Mombasa, by each of the cultural elements represented here. The city will be viewed in two ways: the first part of the book will consist of a general, functional approach to the occupation of the entire site (island as well as mainland); the latter chapters will focus on the characteristics of that area where the various cultural elements are drawn most closely together, the CBD.

8. H. J. de Blij, *Dar es Salaam, a Study in Urban Geography* (Evanston, Ill., 1963).

FIGURE 5. A detail of some of the more elaborate memorials. The graves are located between Old Town residences; the waters of Mombasa Harbor can be seen on the right in both photographs.

THE METHOD OF APPROACH

Among the problems related to this work is the paucity of published material dealing specifically with the functional structure of African cities; in the case of Mombasa the available literature deals almost exclusively with history, although there are some sociological studies in addition (see the Bibliography, pp. 158). Nevertheless, more background material is available for Mombasa than was the case for Dar es Salaam, so that the present record is somewhat more complete.

The answers to the more specific questions raised above can only be determined through the interpretation of maps showing the functional elements of the city and the retail structure of the CBD. Data for the construction of these maps were gathered in the field. A considerable amount of incidental information, deemed useful in the analysis, also was recorded in Mombasa. Air photographs were employed to verify field observations, and base maps constructed by the Kenya Survey were used. At a time of transition such as Kenya was experiencing during the course of this study, it is sometimes difficult (and occasionally impossible) to obtain needed data. In Mombasa, as in Lourenço Marques—but for different reasons—the major problem in this area was related to the lack of ready availability of land in the central city.

It is natural, as these studies progress, for comparisons to emerge between the work at hand and previously completed cases. Such comparisons often prove to be fruitful exercises, as was proved in an interim report on the present research.[9] Occasional reference will therefore be made in this study to certain comparative aspects of Dar es Salaam and Lourenço Marques.

9. H. J. de Blij, "Urban Centers in East Africa: Some Comparisons" (abstract), *Program of the 9th Annual Meeting*, African Studies Association, October, 1966, p. 9.

Chapter 2 SITE AND HISTORICAL GEOGRAPHY

MOMBASA'S ORIGINS are shrouded in myth and legend, and doubt has been cast even on the uncertain story of the town's Persian beginnings, a thousand years ago. Some believe that the earliest reference to a settlement on the site of Mombasa was made by Ptolemy in 150 A.D., when he described the existence of a place called Tonika. Quite possibly there were coastal settlements in East Africa at that time, and Mombasa may have been one of them, but it has not been possible to identify the town in the historical record prior to the tenth century with absolute certainty.

There is no doubt, however, that Mombasa played a role in coastal East Africa after the rise of Islam and its arrival on these shores. Whether founded by Persians or Arabs (the Chronicles of

Kilwa relate that it was a grandson of the Sultan of Shiraz who selected the site), a new phase in the history of Mombasa began during the tenth century. And whether a settlement was indeed created or an existing village occupied by the invaders, Mombasa as a result of these attentions became a town to be reckoned with in the centuries that followed. Whoever came first, the Arabs and the Persians both contributed to the development of the site. The town, to some extent protected by minor fortifications, took on the appearance of similar settlements in the colonizers' homelands: narrow, alley-like streets were flanked by solid houses built with local stone and a form of cement, and doors were carved into veritable ornaments, decorated with a variety of metals. Windows were generally quite small and protected by wooden shutters. There were courtyards and well-kept gardens, beautifully inlaid floors, and busy markets. The scene was dominated by mosques, and a busy dhow traffic maintained connections with the outside world (Fig. 6).

Foreign trade was nothing new for East African settlements, and in this respect the Arabs and Persians provided a stimulus but not an innovation. For centuries before the Islamic invasion, the monsoon had been guiding sailing vessels from the coasts of India and Ceylon to Zanzibar, Mogadishu, and other East African settlements, thence to the Arabian Peninsula, the home base, and on to southern Asia. The Chinese contributed to this trade as well as the Indians and Arabs; quantities of Chinese pottery and coins have been found along the entire East African coast and even far inland. Indeed, East Africa in a way was an extension of India and southern Asia rather than the continent of which it formed a physical part, and when the Islamic Arab-Persian invasion of the tenth century occurred and additional settlements were founded, there was little change in this pattern. The new foreigners no more intended to colonize the interior than did their predecessors; rather, they intensified the trade pattern already existing, using African middlemen in the coastal hinterland to achieve their ends.

What were the early objects of trade? Again, the pattern had been set long before Mombasa arose to prominence: East Africa was for centuries a ready source of slaves, and it was a veritable mine for ivory. These were the major trading items at the pictur-

FIGURE 6. A view in the Old Town of Mombasa, showing one of the older mosques, a narrow, winding street, and the shuttered windows of adjoining buildings. Corrugated iron sheeting forms the majority of the roofing material today.

esque markets along the coast, and as long as they were produced, supplies arrived in quantity to keep the settlements thriving. Cloth, beads, and metal objects, as well as salt, were brought to East Africa and found their way inland, while in addition to slaves and ivory, some gold and a few spices reached the coast from the interior, to be shipped to the Arab world.

For five centuries Mombasa held its place among the other trading stations along the East African coast. Legend has it that Pata,

Lamu, Malindi, and Kilwa were founded at the same time as Mombasa, but time soon eroded the familial ties that bound them at their birth. A kind of feudalism began to afflict the coast, and an erosive series of struggles ensued, during which various places were supreme at various times, while the others suffered under the heel of ruthless and sometimes savage domination. Much destruction occurred when struggles for power erupted into armed hostilities. Though Mombasa was dominant, especially during the twelfth century, it was involved in a constant rivalry with its northern neighbor, Malindi. When, in 1498, Vasco da Gama arrived to herald the period of Portuguese involvement, he called at both Mombasa and Malindi, but Malindi was then the more powerful and prosperous town.

THE SITE

The entire coast of East Africa has undergone submergence during recent geologic times, and, as is characteristic of such shorelines, there are numerous small islands, narrow drowned valleys representing the lower parts of former river courses, and shallow coral reefs. It was upon one of these many islands that the city of Mombasa was founded, although the urban area today sprawls onto the mainland in several directions. A number of Mombasa's former competitors also were established on island sites: Lamu, Pata, and Kilwa are among them.

The islands afforded the Arab-Persian traders several advantages. Quite apart from the natural protection against any potential mainland threats, many of the islands provided fresh-water wells and some areas of adequate soil for the cultivation of staple crops. With their hard-rock base and coral fringes, building materials for the kinds of structures the Arabs built were easily obtained. Most important of all was the fact that by the very nature of their origins, such islands were flanked by waters sufficiently deep and yet well enough protected to provide good harbor facilities. The Arab dhow plying the East African coast was—and remains—a vessel of relatively small size and draft, and it could enter many small harbors quite easily (Fig. 7).

FIGURE 7. Although the monsoon winds bring the dhow fleet to Mombasa Harbor between January and April, other small schooners, employing sail as well as engine, manage to ply the East African coast from Lamu to Lindi all the year around (with a midyear interruption to allow the storms of that period to pass). Shown here are several such small coastal boats in Mombasa Harbor, at the foot of Old Town. (Quality Photo Process)

Mombasa Island is some 3 miles in length and averages less than 2 miles in width (Fig. 8). Its long axis trends northwest-southeast, and the island tapers slightly toward the Indian Ocean. The total area is somewhat over 5 square miles, but the area presently covered by the municipality of Mombasa is nearly 75 square miles. Ocean-going vessels can approach the island through a gap measuring 1.6 miles between the coral reefs which lie off two adjacent headlands, Leven Reef (off Nyali to the north) and Andromache Reef (off Likoni to the south) (Fig. 9).

The story of the decline of several of Mombasa's competitors is related to the arrival of the steamship era, the need for deeper waters and better harbor entrance and access facilities, and the

FIGURE 8.   Vertical air photograph showing Mombasa Island and adjacent mainland areas. (Courtesy Kenya Survey Office)

unavailability of such advantages at the local sites. Mombasa was fortunate. For centuries development here was based upon the use of Mombasa Harbor, which lies to the east of the island and which has an entrance channel averaging 300 yards in width. This harbor came into use not because it afforded the only possible site for this purpose, but because the channel off the western side of the island presented difficulties for sailing ships in terms of prevailing wind directions and current velocities. When the new era in navigation arrived and ships grew larger and independent of wind and current, the western channel proved more suitable for modern development, and Mombasa found it possessed the opportunities the other sites so often lacked.

Mombasa Harbor, however, was for centuries the place of call for thousands of dhows (and it serves coastal vessels of this type to

FIGURE 9. Andromache Reef (*A*) and the entrance to Kilindini Harbor. The photograph looks toward the southeast from the southernmost corner of Mombasa Island.

the present day). Hence urban development took place first on the margins of this port, and it was the eastern and southeastern part of the island that saw the rise of Old Mombasa.[1] Mombasa Harbor, which is somewhat shallower than the western channel named Kilindini Harbor, also is rather more exposed to the ocean. Northward, after several tortuous bends, the channel widens into what has long been known as Port Tudor. Navigational difficulties have precluded the use and development of this harbor, and at present most of it is closed off by a low-level bridge connecting the island to the northern mainland.

Kilindini Harbor not only proved capable of accommodating modern ships, but its northward extension, Port Reitz, was found to be suitable for further development when Kilindini Harbor was

1. There is a tradition which suggests that a settlement existed on the western side of the island, near the modern port, before Mombasa arose to the east. Indeed, ruins have been found in the area, though they are as yet undated.

taxed to capacity. At present the mile-long quay of Kilindini Harbor is being supplemented by a new wharf on the mainland; the initial stages of development can be observed at A on Figure 8.

In terms of relief, Mombasa Island is quite flat, with the exception of a rather prominent bluff around the margins and some associated undulations. Terrain, in any event, has not been a major obstacle in the development of the city, although, as will be seen

FIGURE 10. A view of the vegetation and terrain of the mainland to the north of Mombasa Island. The slope areas are affected by erosion, but on the terrace surface the vegetation is quite dense. The view is toward Changamwe.

later, the waterways described in the preceding paragraphs did play a role in urban fragmentation when the sprawl onto the mainland began. The original vegetation has been largely destroyed, but a glimpse of it can still be caught in some remnants in the northeastern one-eighth of the island, where the last bit of unoccupied land is just being invaded by permanent buildings. The adjacent mainland reveals the appearance much of the island must have had at one time: a fairly dense growth of coconut palms and other trees, with grass of medium height (Fig. 10).

THE SEQUENCE OF OCCUPATION

The first Arab-Persian occupants of Mombasa Island knew little of the potential value of the site they had selected for their trading station. The Old Town grew slowly, and at times the population even declined with its varying fortunes. Much of the island was planted with citrus trees and coconut palms, and the settlement attracted some Africans from the mainland (other than the slaves already working the farms and serving families in the town). Indeed, during this early period of Arab-Persian immigration there was undoubtedly a certain amount of intermarriage with African residents of the area, a factor which is of significance in the continuing social relationships among the many racial groups occupying Mombasa today.

This, the first Arab period of domination at Mombasa, was terminated shortly after the arrival of Vasco da Gama. The fall of Mombasa to the Portuguese was in part due to the continuing rivalry with Malindi, for Malindi by 1505 had aligned itself with the European invaders and received a share of the profits when Mombasa fell. But Mombasa, no easy prize during the days of interfamily feudalism, proved an obstinate ward of the Portuguese as well. It harassed the new colonizers and provoked them into another destructive attack in 1528. Later it accepted the assistance of new arrivals on the East African scene, the Turks, but in 1589 the Portuguese, this time assisted by a force of mainland African allies, captured the Turkish fleet and smashed the town's opposition.

Now the Portuguese chose Mombasa as their headquarters and decided upon the move from Malindi, planning at the same time to build an impregnable fort overlooking Mombasa Harbor. Fort Jesus was begun in 1593, but the Portuguese failed to come to terms with the Sultan, who was murdered at their behest in 1614. In 1631 the Sultan's son brought on a revolt which led to the massscre of all but five of the Portuguese detachment then at Mombasa, but in 1639 the Portuguese once again captured the city and began to rebuild Fort Jesus (Figs. 11, 12).

FIGURE 11. Fort Jesus, now a museum and in the process of restoration, for many years served as the jail of Mombasa. It is still one of the largest structures in the city, and in the photograph it looms over Mombasa Harbor.

The days of the Portuguese in this part of East Africa, however, were numbered. The Arabian state of Oman, rapidly growing in power, was beginning to drive the Portuguese from the Arabian coasts. Mombasa once again grew restive, and appeals went out to Oman for aid in ousting the Portuguese. By the middle of the century the Omani challenged the Portuguese at Pata and Zanzibar and forced them from these strongholds, and in 1660 they drove the Europeans out of Mombasa Town, although Fort Jesus held fast. For over thirty years the two powers were involved in an uneasy standoff, but finally the confrontation came. In 1696 the Omani laid siege to Fort Jesus and maintained it for 33 months. Finally the Portuguese garrison collapsed as the fort was stormed.

The end of Portuguese control at Fort Jesus signaled the beginning of a lengthy interruption of European domination along the entire East African coast. While the Portuguese withdrew to Moçambique, neither the Hollanders nor the British replaced them,

FIGURE 12. Fort Jesus saw centuries of history, and many different flags flew from its towers. After the first period of construction by the Portuguese, which began in 1593, the fort was repeatedly strengthened. Two building phases are seen in this photograph, a detail of the wall at *A* in Figure 11.

and so another century of Arab hegemony occurred, interrupted only by one last Portuguese effort to regain Fort Jesus (1728–30). But once again the Arabs failed to keep the peace among themselves. Naturally Oman claimed supremacy at Mombasa, but in 1741 Mombasa declared itself independent. Thus began one of the most influential periods in the city's history, as Malindi fell under its sway along with some 150 miles of coastline including the port of Pangani and a section of the island of Pemba. Eventually the Imam of Oman, Seyyid Said, challenged the independence of the East African coastal towns and began to take action against them. In this he was supported—or at least not obstructed—by the British, who saw in him an opportunity to achieve their new goal in East Africa, the termination of the slave trade.

Facing the challenge of Oman, Mombasa had sought aid from the British, but the British were reluctant to jeopardize their good relationship with Said; in fact they signed a treaty in 1822 which in effect recognized the Imam's hegemony over the East African coast. But Mombasa's persistent desire to enlist British aid led to one of those accidents that make history. Late in 1823 the British fleet, operating against the slave trade, entered Mombasa Harbor. The leaders of the Mombasa community—the powerful Mazrui family —requested permission to hoist the British flag over the town and the fort, as a sign of identification with and support from Britain. Indeed, they had already manufactured such a flag. Apparently no decision was made by the British commander at that time. But when the same fleet returned to Mombasa three months later, they found hostilities in progress—the Omani fleet was attacking Fort Jesus, from whose tower flew the British flag. This time there was no hesitation; shortly afterward a British protectorate was created at Mombasa, in return for a Mazrui promise that the slave trade there would be terminated.

The first protectorate at Mombasa was of brief duration, for the Mazrui soon behaved toward their British protectors as they had toward Oman shortly after the defeat of the Portuguese. By 1826 the British had given up hope of a lasting accommodation here, and they withdrew the small garrison that had been left at the fort. Said did not hesitate long, and the next year his fleet again bombarded Mombasa. But it was not until ten years later, and then only because of internal rivalries and corruption within Mombasa, that Said was able to enter and make Omani supremacy a fact.

Having finally taken Mombasa and Fort Jesus, Seyyid Said transferred his ruling headquarters from Muscat in Arabia to Zanzibar. He appointed a governor to rule Mombasa, but the relationships between Zanzibari authority and the government at Mombasa were not always good. Upon his death in 1856, Said's possessions in Oman and East Africa were divided between his sons, Majid and Thuwaini, and a new struggle resulted. This period witnessed a precipitous decline in the influence and stature of Mombasa and a corresponding rise to prominence of Zanzibar. Just as Mombasa's rise under Portuguese hegemony was attended by a disastrous exodus from Malindi, so the present ascent of Zanzibar led to a calamitous evacuation of Mombasa Town. Almost all influence in the inland areas was lost. African tribesmen held sway to within a few miles of the settlement. Arab, Swahili, and Asian traders and craftsmen departed by the hundreds. By 1880 the place was in decay, a mere shadow of its former eminence and prosperity.

Even now the events which brought Mombasa its twentieth-century success were but barely foreshadowed. While some missionaries were active in the general attempt to end slavery on the island (Freretown was established in the mid-1870's as a haven for freed slaves) the British government focused its attention upon the sultans of Zanzibar as the greatest hope for success in this venture. Seyyid Majid was succeeded in 1870 by Seyyid Bargash, and during his rule slavery was rendered illegal throughout the dominions ruled from the island. Zanzibar's market was officially closed in 1873, but in Mombasa, predictably, there were problems. The Arabs regarded the existence of Freretown and other centers for the betterment of freed slaves as a provocation, and in 1880 the first organized attack upon Freretown took place. This series of hostilities did not end until 1896.

Meanwhile, British occupation with the problems of the slave trade and the relationships with Zanzibar was rudely disturbed by the entry of Germany onto the East African colonial stage. The new competition led to the first semilegal delimitation of the sultan's mainland possessions, which by an international commission in 1886 were adjudged to consist of a strip of land, ten miles wide, along the coast. The strip was divided between the Germans, who took possession of it to the south of the town of Vanga, and the British, who in 1887 placed a British East Africa Association in charge of Sultan Bargash's fifty-year concession over the ten-mile strip from Vanga north to Kipini. The next year this association was granted a royal charter and became the Imperial British East Africa Company. Its major asset—and liability—was the town of Mombasa.

The first seven years of British administration at Mombasa produced little but failures. The company simply did not have the resources required to perform its administrative and rehabilitative tasks; it was beleaguered by continued internal quarreling and strife within Mombasa, and while it recognized the need for effective communications with a possibly lucrative hinterland, it did not have the finances to construct them. Ultimately it was forced to appeal to both the British public and the British government for assistance. The end was not long in coming, and in mid-1895 the Union Jack came to replace the company's banner on official buildings. Thus came about the British East Africa Protectorate, still nominally a part of Zanzibar and consisting of a strip of land 52 miles long and 10 miles wide which included the still-dormant port of Mombasa.

BRITISH OBJECTIVES

Even as late as 1895, the slave trade and the practice of slavery were not abolished to the satisfaction of the British. Neither had the take-over of the coastal strip solved the financial problems with which this new possession confronted the government. Additionally, there lay in the distant interior, behind Mombasa, a relatively wealthy kingdom on the northern shores of Lake Victoria— Buganda, upon which the covetous eyes of several rival colonial powers were focused. All three of these realities appeared to demand a single effective solution: the construction of a railroad from Mombasa Island, across Kenya, through the Highlands, to Lake Victoria, and eventually into Buganda itself. The first rails were laid down at Kilindini in 1896, and in late 1901 the connection to Kisumu on Lake Victoria was completed.[2]

While the struggle against the slave trade met with success and Uganda became a British protectorate, the matter of finances remained a major problem. British East Africa did not produce the mineral deposits of South Africa or the quick agricultural opportunities of West Africa. Hence the decision was made to attract white settlers to those regions deemed suitable for cash agriculture, notably the region of the Kenya Highlands, in the hope that export production and import demands would repay the debts incurred through the building of the Uganda Railway. That objective, too, was achieved, and in the process Mombasa, which just decades

2. For details concerning these developments see M. F. Hill, *Permanent Way* (Nairobi, 1951–58), Vol. I: *East African Railways and Harbours*. Vol. II also contains a considerable amount of incidental information.

earlier was being eclipsed by such places as Bagamoyo and Zanzibar, reached an unprecedented rate of growth and expansion.

THE IMPACT: THE RISE OF MODERN MOMBASA

Old Mombasa never came close to filling the available area on the island. Until late in the nineteenth century the town probably never exceeded a half square mile in total area, and the correct figure may be nearer a quarter of a square mile. Congested as it was, the walled town never sprawled outward along finger-like arteries; immediately beyond the walls were the gardens and plantations which provided the immediate need for foodstuffs. The largest structure was towering Fort Jesus, from whose embankments the town could be overlooked. The port remained primitive, with few facilities to ease the handling of goods and cargo. The Arabs and Persians had brought to the town the architectural know-how of their homelands, and the town they created was an imitation of what existed there. By contemporary standards, though, Mombasa was by no means an insignificant place; many travelers described their admiration for the size, wealth, and organization of the settlement.

The coming of British administration in Mombasa was attended by many immediate and momentous changes. Many of these, as will shortly be shown, were reflected in the urban landscape and the whole organization of the island. But there were others of equal significance. Until the late nineteenth century Mombasa had been an Arab town in the true sense of the word; indeed, in some ways the great influence of the most prominent Arab family there made it seem like a Mazrui town. There was mixture with Africans, true, and there were Asians from south Asia engaged in trade, commerce, and the real estate business. But the tenor of the town was an Arab one: the important decisions were made by Arabs, and the practice of slavery kept Africans other than middlemen away unless they were linked to families by history or trade. All this came to an end with the arrival of the British. A rapid influx of population began, the bulk of which was non-Arab. Slavery was abolished, and

Africans flooded the free settlements and the island in search of work. Europeans came in large numbers, and their administration terminated old practices and instituted new ones. When the building of the railroad began, high wages attracted thousands of Africans to the site, and as it progressed, a wave of Indian labor, imported by the British, began to arrive at Mombasa. Soon the Arabs found themselves to be a small and rather insignificant minority, still centered upon the Old Town, not participating in these new developments to any real degree, and faced with a loss of the stature and privileges which formerly had been commonplace.

This sequence of events at Mombasa, of course, was not unique in East Africa, though some of the old trading stations, for example Lamu, remained dominantly Arab towns as they were before the invasion of Europe. Generally the arrival of the British (and the Germans, initially, in what is today Tanzania) changed completely the manner in which the settlements were organized and administered, with an almost complete loss of power on the part of those who had held sway just years earlier. The extent to which Arabs have been relegated to a minority in both Mombasa and Dar es Salaam is illustrated by Table 1.

TABLE 1 *

Racial Communities in Dar es Salaam and Mombasa, 1957–58

	Dar es Salaam 1957	Mombasa 1958
Africans	94,000	90,000
Asians (including Goans)	28,000	27,500
Arabs	2,500	19,000
Whites	4,500	4,400

* Both sets of figures are rounded off from census data for those years. For a discussion of some general aspects of the demography of Dar es Salaam, see the *Tanganyika Standard,* June 21, 1961.

None of the racial communities in Mombasa is unified and homogeneous. The relatively small Arab community, still centered today in the Old Town, is classified into four major groups, a division which is based upon their historical ties with the place and the time of their forebears' arrival. The so-called "twelve tribes" trace their arrival to the first period of Arab hegemony after the rise of Islam. A second group, the Mazrui, numbers seventeen "tribes" and dates its arrival during the period of Omani supremacy following the ouster of the Portuguese. A third group is constituted of merchants, traders, and sailors, all of whom arrived but a short time ago. Some of these newcomers still travel the monsoonal paths of the dhows, while considering Mombasa their home base. Finally there are the Sharifs, families claiming ties with the Prophet, who stand aloof from the others. Many of them have resided in Mombasa for centuries.

The Arab groups, especially those who have been on the coast for many centuries, have undergone admixture with the Africans. Indeed, the first group, the twelve tribes, identify themselves as Afro-Asians (another name often given them is Swahili). For several reasons, there is some tension, a certain latent friction, among Arab families in Mombasa, and a strict social order governs individual relationships. To some degree the older Arab families of Mombasa dislike the more recent traders and laborers, who have not yet developed sufficient loyalty to the community and make little contribution. The general decline in wealth has not helped matters, although a tenacious effort is made to retain as much of the Arab culture as possible. In the mosques, schools, and modest homes the pride of the community is still reflected, the difficulties of the times notwithstanding (Fig. 13).

These difficulties are not confined to the loss of status and privilege. Those Arabs who managed to fit themselves into the new colonial pattern often found that more subtle disadvantages now faced them. Some opened shops, while a few entered the wholesale trade. But here they faced the formidable competition of the Indians, who carefully, and to some degree with the help of the colonial administration, protected their advantageous position. These Indians had been trading in Mombasa for generations, and the entry of Arabs into this field was not always welcomed. Now the Arabs were the latecomers, and the Indians successfully used the historical argument to obtain protection from the British.

The larger Asian community of Mombasa is also divided. The

Figure 13. The impressive Mbaruk Mosque on Jivanjee Street in the Old Town. Like many mosques in Mombasa, this structure is in excellent condition as a result of the continuous care and investment of the religious community.

broadest possible classification is into three categories: a grouping of Hindu communities, a set of Muslim communities, and a Goan community. There are today perhaps 40,000 Asians in Mombasa, of whom, if previous figures may be extrapolated, some 21,000 are Hindus and 15,000 are Muslims. The majority of the remainder are Goans.[3]

Although an influx of Asian labor accompanied the construction of the Uganda Railway, Indian and other Asian families had been on the East African coast for many generations prior to that time. Although, for example, most Goan families arrived after 1895, the first Goans to reach East Africa came during the period of Portuguese involvement along these shores, which began in the early 1500's and ended in 1730. An Ismaili community existed at Baga-

3. For details, based upon the 1958 census, see G. M. Wilson, "Mombasa—A Modern Colonial Municipality," in A. Southall, Social Change in Modern Africa (London, 1961), p. 100.

moyo in 1815 (though representatives did not come to Mombasa until 1900), and from Zanzibar members of the Dawoodi-Bohra Muslims came in 1880. The Bhadala community was established at Zanzibar in 1705, and the dhows brought them as well as others to Mombasa Town.[4]

The fragmentation of the Asian community is reflected by the many individual units identified within it, among them the Parsis, the six hundred Patel families, the Sikhs, and a host of others. Many of these units have their own schools, cemeteries, and religious buildings, and this duplication makes a considerable impact upon the townscape (Figs. 14, 15). In contrast to the Arab community, the Asians possess considerable wealth, and their dominance of the commercial life of this city and others need not be emphasized.

The African population resident within the Mombasa municipality now numbers well in excess of 100,000 (Table 2). As in all urban centers of subsaharan Africa, this urbanized population is still divided by its tribal associations, language, custom barriers, and so forth. Although the great influx to Mombasa has taken place during the present century, there have always been some Africans at the site. As mentioned previously, Arabs occasionally took African women as wives, and a relatively small population of servants and laborers attended the Arab families of Old Mombasa. The slave trade, and the practice of slavery itself which was carried on at Mombasa, also brought Africans to the site. When the first free place for released slaves was created (during the brief "protectorate" of Captain Owen, in the early 1820's) at English Point across Mombasa Harbor, the future was foreshadowed. Later, slaves freed in Mombasa and the adjacent mainland settled in more permanent refuges such as Freretown, and hundreds of others arrived from up-country and elsewhere along the coast. There were some calls that the tide be stemmed, but soon another invasion began. Not only did the wages paid by the railroad construction jobs attract many more settlers, but the railroad itself channeled Africans toward Mombasa. Each time the railway reached a new tribal area, representatives of that tribal people began to arrive in Mombasa in

4. *Ibid.*, p. 101.

FIGURE 14. Many Asian communities in Mombasa have their own religious temples and shrines. This Cutch Temple is located along Haile Selassie Road and reflects the wealth of the community it serves.

FIGURE 15. Lord Shiva Temple, a Hindu shrine on the southern edge of Old Town. This is an elaborate structure, in contrast to many modest mosques in the nearby streets of Old Mombasa.

search of jobs. Even Kikuyu and Luo came from afar, as had the Kamba and Taita earlier.

The accommodation of this flood of African labor provided Mombasa with one of its major social problems, although, as will be suggested in Chapter 3, the situation might have been a great deal worse than it was. Very few real slums developed in the town, and even today there is nothing to rival the deterioration so common in many cities of equal size.

TABLE 2 *

African Population of Mombasa District

		Not Stated	1,059
BANTU	Central Bantu	Kikuyu	8,094
		Embu	475
		Meru	634
		Mbere	95
		Kamba	16,767
		Tharaka	247
	Western Bantu	Luhya	7,272
		Kisii	163
		Kuria	109
	Coastal Bantu	Mijikenda	42,017
		Pokomo/Riverine	1,030
		Taveta	92
		Taita	8,535
		Swahili/Shirazi	2,793
		Bajun	1,000
		Boni/Sanya	38
	Nilotic	Luo	10,875
NILO-HAMITIC	Nilo-Hamitic Kalenjin-speaking	Nandi	327
		Kipsigis	115
		Elgeyo	36
		Marakwet	26
		Pokot	8
		Tugen	16
	Other Nilo-Hamitic	Masai	117
		Samburu	16
		Turkana	37
		Iteso	81
		Nderobo	7
		Njemps	2

* *Kenya Population Census, 1962,* Economics and Statistics Division, Ministry of Finance and Economic Planning (Kenya, 1964), p. 60. The tribal classification that forms the basis for the census is given on p. 2.

TABLE 2 (Continued)

African Population of Mombasa District

HAMITIC	*Western Hamitic* *Rendille & Galla* *speaking*	Rendille	1
		Boran	29
		Gabbra	9
		Sakuye	3
		Orma	44
	Eastern Hamitic *Somali-speaking*	Hawiyah	37
		Ogaden	14
		Gurreh	1
		Other Somali	267
	Foreign African	Tanganyika	6,605
		Uganda	1,542
		Sudan	240
		Ethiopia	45
		Malawi, Rhodesia, Zambia	775
		Rwanda, Burundi	33
		Other African Countries	119
		Total District Mombasa	111,847

The whites or Europeans who came to Mombasa with the British take-over also had various backgrounds, aspirations, and roles to play. Hence they, too, failed to form a truly homogeneous community, although their position of power elevated them to the top of the social pyramid. With the British East Africa Association and the Royal Company came officials and administrators, civil servants, and others in governmental or municipal employ. As the town grew and acquired its new image, more and more professional people and businessmen came to take up permanent residence. In addition, Mombasa, like every other colonial town, attracted many temporary residents, who, in periodic contract work or other short-term employment, spent periods from weeks to years in the town. Therefore, the effective European population, that is, the population who played a role in improving race relations and developing the town's potential, and who invested the better part of a lifetime in the process, was always considerably smaller than the census figures suggest.

At first, the Europeans found themselves in the ancient town without adequate accommodations and facilities. The British East Africa Association had made relatively little impact on the site, though it had constructed a residence for the chief administrator at Kilindini in 1890. But many of the lesser officials were forced to live for some time in temporary accommodations on the Ndia Kuu, the main street of Old Town, while others lived in tents.

The establishment of the protectorate increased the pace of progress. Those in charge of the construction of the Uganda Railway now also required accommodation, and building began. Banks opened offices in the town; the National Bank of India and the Chartered Bank were the first. Consumer goods were required in growing quantity, and foreign firms established branches at Mombasa. New quarters were built for the administration, and to the west and south of Fort Jesus a cluster of government buildings arose, of which several are still in use today (Fig. 16).

During the mid-1890's a decision was made which completely

FIGURE 16. The British contribution: a government building on Treasury Square, within a few hundred feet of Fort Jesus. The center of the Kenya Coast Authority is today housed in these structures; not far to the south is the President's House, and nearby are the Town Hall and the Lands and Survey Offices. The building shown here is located just across from the southern edge of the Old Town and leaves little doubt regarding the origins of its architecture and style.

altered the direction in which Mombasa Town had been developing. The increased flow of goods, the growing difficulties in handling bulky cargo, and the endless congestion and confusion in Mombasa Harbor led to the abandonment of this port in favor of Kilindini, on the opposite side of the island, where better opportunities existed for the development of a modern port. This meant that the focus of activity shifted completely, and such facilities as Mombasa Harbor did possess—and there were some, including on-shore ware-houses—found themselves left behind in the rush to the new port site. The railway, too, led from Kilindini to the mainland, though the station was positioned approximately in the center of the island and a major road was laid out to connect it to Old Town. Long known as Station Road, this artery is today called Haile Selassie Avenue.

The railroad, of course, required that a permanent connection be built between the island and the mainland. A temporary structure was erected in 1896 to function as a bridge to the northern main-land, and in 1901 the more permanent Makupa Causeway was officially opened. Later this viaduct was further improved, first in 1929 when a road-rail bridge was completed, and subsequently in the mid-1960's when a four-lane highway was laid adjacent to the railroad lines.

Despite the recent rapid growth of the municipal population resident on the mainland, Mombasa Island is connected with its adjacent areas in only two other places, one of which serves only as a port connector. The Kipevu Causeway links Kilindini Harbor with Port Reitz. The other structure is a privately constructed pon-toon bridge, reputed to be the largest of its kind in the world. Built in the 1930's by Nyali Ltd., this toll bridge joins Mombasa Island to a high-class residential estate (still being developed by Nyali), the newly developing Kisauni Point, and the older settlements of Kis-auni and Freretown. The only remaining link of major consequence (apart from unscheduled ferries such as Mtongwe and Kisauni) is that across the entrance of Kilindini Harbor. This is the Likoni Ferry, and its capacities are increasingly taxed by the traffic volume between Mombasa and the inland and coastal south (Figs. 17, 18, 19). A low-level bridge cannot be built here, of course, and until

FIGURES 17, 18, 19. The only effective link between Mombasa Island
and both the southern parts of the municipality and the Kenya South
Coast is the Likoni Ferry, shown in these photographs. The line of
vehicles awaiting the arrival of the ferry on the mainland (Fig. 17)
promises a lengthy wait for those toward the rear; the capacity of the
crowded ferry shown arriving from the island (Fig. 18) is limited.
Peak-hour departures occur every twenty minutes, and many commuters
travel on foot or by bicycle (Fig. 19).

now the costs of a high-level or drawbridge have been prohibitive.
There can be no doubt, however, that residential development at
Likoni has been hindered by the inadequacies of the Likoni Ferry,
and even the improvements in equipment and timetables, instituted
recently, cannot provide a substitute for a bridge or causeway. In
effect, then, Mombasa Island has but one really good connection
with the mainland, and this is the Makupa Causeway to the northwest.

But in the early 1900's the island was far from occupied, there was no land pressure other than that which Old Town imposed upon itself, and a town plan could be laid out which provided ample space for all functional areas of the urban unit. For a brief period, from 1900 to 1905, Mombasa was the capital of mainland British East Africa, until the decision was made to move the governmental headquarters to Nairobi. During the next several decades Mombasa was the pulse of its hinterland. Rising hopes of spectacular achievements in the interior were reflected by periods of building activity in the port. The construction of a small pier in Kilindini Harbor was followed in 1907 by the building of a lighterage wharf, when expectations for cotton cultivation in Uganda and white settler agriculture in the Highlands were great. In 1913 a private company built another pier for the handling of salt traffic. After the First World War the modern port really began to take shape. In 1921 work was started on the first of the deep-water berths, and by 1958 the entire available frontage was occupied by a mile-long quay. The need had arisen for further development on the mainland, at Port Reitz.

One major consequence of the westward shift of the focus of activity on the island relates to the survival of so much of Old Town. Other coastal places, such as Lourenço Marques and, to a lesser degree, Dar es Salaam, possessed Old Town areas which were located, naturally, in close proximity to the functioning port. When modernization of the port took place, and the pace of change accelerated, these areas were encroached upon by the new central business district, and much of this legacy disappeared. In Lourenço Marques in 1960, modern, multistory structures were rising above the two-level buildings of the Old Town, and without doubt the entire area will be replaced. But in Mombasa there was no need to modernize the foreshore, since the new port lay on the other side of the island, and entirely new facilities could be built there on practically empty ground. Thus a central business district developed, partially pulled to the new area of activity along the Kilindini artery (for street names see Map 6) and partially attracted by the existing business area of the Old Town. Hence the modern and the old business areas have developed adjacent to each other, and very

FIGURE 20. Air photograph showing the Old Town area (A), adjacent
to which lies the modern CBD (B). The major artery just below B,
separating the Old Town from the modern area, is Salim Road. Nyali
Bridge is at C, and D marks the harbor for the dhow traffic (Mombasa
Harbor). The arrow indicates the position of Fort Jesus. (Kenya Government)

FIGURE 21. This photograph shows in part the same area covered in Figure 20. The letters correspond: the Old Town is at *A*, and the CBD lies at *B*. Nyali Bridge is identified by *C*, and *D* marks Mombasa Harbor. Kilindini Harbor lies just beyond the arrow (*E*). Andromache Reef is clearly visible (F), and the area beyond the island is Likoni (*G*). (Quality Photo Process)

little actual replacement has taken place. The situation can be interpreted from Figures 20 and 21; on both illustrations, *A* marks the Old Town area, and *B* is the modern CBD.

As the city developed, a pattern of racial and functional accommodation, the subject of the next chapter, evolved on the island. For years the island was sufficiently large to permit all those who so desired to live there; those who did choose a residence on the mainland did so mostly to escape the bustling city (Nyali Estates, for example, provided the opportunity) or to combine some agriculture with the week's paid work. But eventually the island became crowded, and the mainland sprawl became a matter of necessity. Unlike Lourenço Marques, where considerable vertical development has marked the response to growth pressures in the central city, Mombasa has developed in a horizontal fashion. Few buildings in the CBD are more than three stories high, but the district is highly attenuated and extends for nearly a mile along one of its arteries, Kilindini Avenue, alone.

In the thousand-year history of Mombasa, then, the past six decades have witnessed the evolution of a coastal trading station into a major port of world significance. The vast majority of Mombasa's present assets are the achievements of only a half century, and development continues.

Chapter 3 SITUATION AND FUNCTIONAL STRUCTURE

THE FIRST EFFECTS of the Uganda Railway upon transport patterns in East Africa were felt almost immediately after it reached Kisumu, on Lake Victoria, in 1901.[1] A small lake steamer whose main port of call at that time was Mwanza in German East Africa had just previously been placed in service. From there, goods had traveled by caravan across the Tanganyika plateau to the former slave port of Bagamoyo. Small as it was, this trade volume soon became diverted toward Mombasa, and the final blow to the promi-

1. For a detailed and comprehensive analysis of the evolution of East African transportation patterns see I. S. van Dongen, *The British East African Transport Complex,* University of Chicago Department of Geography Research Papers no. 38 (Chicago, 1954).

nence of Bagamoyo came when the Germans chose Dar es Salaam as their future headquarters.

Both the British and the Germans considered Lake Victoria and Buganda the objective of their East African rail building. Having reached the lake region first, the British were quick to consolidate their advantage. Rail construction soon tied the large navigable Lake Kyoga to Lake Victoria, and the waterways of Lake Albert and the Albert Nile were linked to Lake Kyoga by means of scheduled road services. Ironically, the Germans had been the first to begin a railroad westward from the coast, but progress was so slow that this line, originating from the northern port of Tanga, reached no farther than Moshi, just over 200 miles away, in 1911. Meanwhile another line was begun from Dar es Salaam, but progress was slow, and it only reached Morogoro in 1907, Tabora in 1912, and Kigoma, on Lake Tanganyika, in 1914, just as the First World War commenced. The Mwanza connection never did materialize during the German period: it was laid down by the British after the war. Therefore, in terms of effective coastal communications, Mombasa held a monopoly for more than a decade, and in terms of proximity its advantage has been permanent.

Having secured the connections in Uganda, the British now moved to improve internal communications in Kenya and to consider branch lines to the main railroad. One such branch linked the salt deposits at Lake Magadi to Konza on the main line, and another, built during the First World War, was to have much significance to Mombasa since it ran from Voi toward Taveta near the border of German East Africa. This Voi-Taveta connector was constructed as a strategic device to facilitate entry into German territory during the hostilities. Construction was continued into German territory, and eventually a link was established with the Tanga-Moshi line the Germans had built earlier. Hence Mombasa was connected to Moshi and the rich agricultural areas around Mount Kilimanjaro, for which, in terms of distance, it was the most convenient port of entry and exit. The British acceptance of a mandate over German East Africa after the war secured Mombasa's favored position: the potentially disruptive political boundary lost its influence, and the wartime railroad remained in place to function in Mombasa's expanding hinterland.

In the years between the two World Wars, the railroad system in this area reached more or less its present structure. The transshipments required to move goods from Uganda through Kisumu to Mombasa were cumbersome and expensive, and thus a railroad link was built from the vicinity of Nakuru, through Eldoret, entering Uganda near Tororo, and eventually continuing on to Kampala. About a decade later, the line was further extended to reach the important copper deposits at Kasese in western Uganda. The complementary road services were also improved, while short branch railroads led into the productive highlands to such places as Nanyuki and Thomson's Falls.

Railroad construction in East Africa then came to a virtual halt until the late 1950's, when further developments of significance to Mombasa's situation occurred. In Uganda, construction of a northern line from Tororo to Gulu was completed, and the line was extended to meet water traffic on the Albert Nile at Pakwach. This was the last in a long series of improvements for the port's position in East Africa, and inevitably some less beneficial changes were to occur. One of these relates to a recapture by Tanzania of the Moshi-Kilimanjaro trade, much of which had gone for decades through Mombasa. In the late 1950's a link between the old Tanga-Moshi line and Dar es Salaam was constructed, and the port at Dar es Salaam was modernized. Thus Tanzania's capacity to handle the trade of this region was increased. Subsequently, political relations between Kenya and Tanzania, after an initial period of post-independence cooperation, have somewhat deteriorated. The political boundary has taken on significance again, and goods traffic on the Voi-Moshi line has reflected the new conditions.

Another potential threat to Mombasa's favored position lies in the construction of modern facilities at Tanzania's lake port of Mwanza. The Mwanza-Tabora rail link has never fulfilled its expectations, and with the improvement of the port of Mwanza Tanzanian hopes are that trade now going via other lake ports and the Uganda Railway to Mombasa may be diverted through Tanzania to

Dar es Salaam. Under normal circumstances, such hopes would not be likely to materialize, for the route is longer and the harbor of Dar es Salaam is by no means without its problems—notably, limited berth space. But again the political factor may come to play a role. For Uganda, the Mwanza-Tabora-Dar es Salaam exit is an alternative to total dependence upon Kenya and Mombasa. And while a loss of the Kilimanjaro-Moshi traffic can be easily absorbed by Mombasa, any major cut in the Uganda traffic would be a serious development for the well-being of the port and rail services.

In recent years, although Mombasa has continued to outrank the combined ports of Tanzania in terms of tonnage handled, a decline can be noted in the volume of exports reaching the port from its hinterland. Imports, on the other hand, have continued to rise sharply (see Table 3).

TABLE 3 *

East African Imports
(in 000 Tons)

		Railed Inland	Railed to Coast
Mombasa	1964	1,465	840
	1965	1,742	711
Dar es Salaam	1964	332	314
	1965	367	356
Tanga	1964	25	126
	1965	29	120

* Data from *Annual Report, 1965: East African Railways and Harbours,* Government Printer (Nairobi, 1966), p. 12.

Again, political factors enter into this picture. A few thousand tons of Congo traffic usually reached Mombasa each year, especially after the Kasese line was completed. Instability in the Congo Republic and government restrictions on cross-border trade in Uganda both contributed to a reduction of several tens of thousands of tons in exports arriving by rail at Mombasa. On the other hand, Dar es Salaam benefited somewhat from a revival of activity along its old and cumbersome route leading to the Katanga: in 1965, inbound traffic increased by 4,000 tons, while Katanga exports rose by 18,000 tons to 57,000.[2]

For many years, Mombasa, unlike Lourenço Marques (among other African ports), had the security of handling trade from within its own area; that is, it did not depend upon the trade of extra-territorial areas. This was especially true while Uganda formed part of a British East African framework, but even now, between 60 and 70 per cent of all goods handled by Mombasa's port have Kenyan origins or destinations. Uganda has led in export volume, especially through the shipment of large amounts of cotton and coffee, but Kenya's imports are far in excess of those of Uganda. Tanzania also has contributed some thousands of tons of coffee from its Bukoba District in the far northwest, across Lake Victoria, but the bulk of Mombasa's trade is Kenyan. This, of course, is one basis for the reputation and growth of the city, which now has a variety of facilities, including a cold store and large bunkering area, which are not available to customers of any of its nearby competitors.

Mombasa's immediate hinterland makes little contribution to the traffic of goods reaching the island; it is estimated that less than 5 per cent of such traffic arrives by means other than rail. Little can be grown in the drier adjacent areas; rainfall decreases greatly away from the coast. Mombasa is an island in more than the real, physiographic sense, for unlike so many of its coastal rivals, it has practically no tributary area where the impact of the urban market nearby has led to developments in agriculture. Even the coast traffic from the north and south coasts, arriving by coastal dhow or schooner or perhaps by truck across the Nyali Bridge or the Likoni Ferry, is of very minor significance. In Tanzania, on the other hand, coastal plantations, especially those under sisal, contribute importantly to the volume of traffic handled at the ports. The contrast is well illustrated by Table 4, which also emphasizes the minor importance of minerals in the export figures for Mombasa and the ports of Tanzania.

The developments summarized above have been mirrored most impressively in Kilindini Harbor itself, where a reclaimed area of

2. *Ibid.*

Table 4 *

Principal Commodities Exported
(In thousand harbor tons: 1 ton = 2,240 lbs.)

	Mombasa		Tanzania Ports	
	1964	1965	1964	1965
Beans, peas and pulses	17,821	13,176	15,116	4,840
Butter	1,645	505	—	—
Cashew nuts	4,190	6,910	51,942	67,343
Cassava	—	—	28,455	7,847
Castor seeds	11,249	8,659	10,212	6,615
Cement, bulk	186,081	237,431	—	—
Cement, bagged	85,155	75,016	—	—
Coffee	243,975	230,219	20,162	20,770
Copper cement	4,323	2,188	13,671	20,333
Copper blister	15,824	16,085	—	—
Copra	—	—	5,174	1,325
Cotton and cotton lint	154,777	172,962	90,741	106,538
Fruit, canned	12,701	11,183	620	123
Grain	5,650	2,444	27,527	241
Groundnuts	5,683	1,480	10,827	6,146
Hides and skins	15,538	18,126	6,638	10,453
Kapok	—	—	3,320	3,614
Meat canned	3,392	4,089	8,574	8,224
Meat chilled or frozen	3,569	3,506	—	—
Oil, lubricating and fuel, cased and drummed	14,542	12,471	513	331
Oil seed and cake	64,771	67,937	36,689	43,179
Pyrethrum	1,987	2,385	507	6,199
Scrap metal	24,508	12,073	6,711	2,769
Sisal	91,365	89,975	336,834	321,452
Soda ash	73,618	69,987	—	—
Tea	68,934	64,991	11,808	18,156
Timber	11,115	11,170	9,740	11,302
Wattle extract	17,718	13,512	8,973	7,610
Wattle bark	6,864	4,610	—	—
Tobacco	—	878	570	4,345
Cotton seeds	—	1	5,145	2,125

* *East African Railways and Harbours,* p. 62.

land below the island bluff has been transformed into a modern, well-planned, and still expanding complex which covers, with its industrial area, nearly one-quarter of the island. The growth of Kilindini, however, was accompanied by the development of a major urban complex, whose elements themselves are a mirror of evolving Kenya.[3]

3. For an extensive discussion of Mombasa's port, trade volume, competitive position, and associated matters see I. S. van Dongen, "Mombasa in the Land and Sea Exchanges of East Africa," *Erdkunde,* XVII (July, 1963), 16–38.

FUNCTIONS

Mombasa's spatial organization naturally reflects the fact that the city constitutes the largest port and second industrial center of Kenya and, indeed, of East Africa. On the island, the largest contiguous functional zone is devoted exclusively to transportation and industry (Map 2). The mainland to the northwest, too, is beginning to feel the impact of these activities.

In general terms, the two salient features of the form and structure of the city are (1) the crowding of so many functional zones on the island and the high density of population there, and (2) the rapid invasion of the adjacent mainland areas, where some organization is being brought to the rather haphazard development of the past. It has been noted previously that urban centers in colonial and recently colonized Africa display a territorial separation of urban functional zones, and that such separation is especially evident in the cities of Africa formerly administered by the British.[4] The island site of Mombasa, however, precluded the convenient establishment of distant high-class residential areas within easy commuting distance of the central city; with improving communications such areas eventually developed, but for decades all major functional zones were contained by the island itself, and none was very far from another. Predictably the most exclusive residential areas that did develop were established in especially suitable areas. In the small ocean-front area in the southeastern corner a zone of first-class residences was built, overlooking the golf course and the ocean. In the far northeast of the island, on its only peninsula of consequence, another fine residential zone developed in the Tudor area opposite Port Tudor. Today, as will be seen later, both areas have been affected by some deterioration.

---

4. In South Africa such separation is one of the fundamentals of urban planning. See B. S. Young, "Some Aspects of the Central Business District of Port Elizabeth, Cape Province," *South African Journal of Social Research,* XII, no. 1 (May, 1961). Portuguese African cities, on the other hand, display the rather close contiguity of functions characteristic also of Portuguese metropolitan towns. Another British-developed city, Dar es Salaam, like Nairobi, shows the wide separation alluded to in H. J. de Blij, *Dar es Salaam, a Study in Urban Geography* (Evanston, Ill., 1963), pp. 27–28.

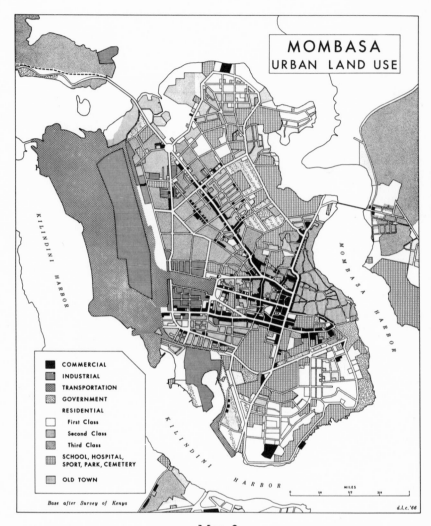

MAP 2

The island-focused urban pattern may well be unique for British-influenced Africa. Residential areas associated to a considerable
extent with individual racial sectors developed in close proximity to
one another, and the realities of space and economics pushed
preferences into the background. Under the circumstances it is not
surprising that the organization of the island shows little regularity.
Although the CBD is centrally located (Map 2), elements of con-

centricity are barely recognizable. Mombasa has a core, but its middle zone (using the usual definitions to characterize this area) is at best intermittently visible. The Old Town, with its warehouses and wholesaling, has some of the aspects normally associated with a middle zone, and to the west of the CBD, near the railroad station,

FIGURE 22. Facing west-southwest from the northern edge of the CBD, this photograph shows the market area (*A*), the vertical development associated with the modern CBD (*B*), and the railroad station (*C*). Just above *C*, the middle zone industrial development west of the CBD can be seen. In the distance (*D*) is Kilindini Harbor, with several ships awaiting berths. (Quality Photo Process)

lies an area of smaller industries (Fig. 22). But both northward and southward, the CBD gives way to dominantly residential areas.

As the island becomes increasingly devoted to transportation, industrial, and commercial activities, and the mainland sprawl continues, a broad concentric pattern may well emerge, in which physiographic features such as the waters of Tudor-Mombasa and Kilindini-Port Reitz, and the smaller creeks cutting the mainland, play their divisive roles. The development of Nyali-Kisauni in the north and Likoni in the south suggests that this will be one aspect of the pattern of the future, while the area farthest from the cool, desirable sites of the north and south mainland, principally Changamwe, will become the main and most populous lower-class residential (and perhaps to some extent industrial) area. The 1958 Mombasa Municipality Census reported a total of nearly 40 per cent of the African population living on the mainland, and in all probability the figure is today in excess of 50 per cent.

Some evidence does exist on Mombasa Island of a sector or pie-shaped arrangement of functional zones. Focusing upon the CBD, there are, starting with Old Town and moving counterclockwise, the large and dominantly Asian-occupied area of second-class homes which extends westward as far as Jomo Kenyatta Avenue (see Map 2 and also Fig. 23), followed by the large third-class

FIGURE 23. This view, westward overlooking the large second-class residential area between Nasser and Kenyatta Avenues, shows clearly the transition between these multistory houses and the single-story dwellings beyond. A line connecting the two arrow points marks the change. Mombasa Municipal Stadium is in the foreground. (Quality Photo Process)

FIGURE 24. A southward view across the first-class residential area, schools, and open ground on the oceanward side of Mombasa Island. Across the entrance to Kilindini Harbor is Likoni. The large school shown is the Star of the Sea, of which the grounds at the left are a part. (Quality Photo Process)

residential area wedged between this artery and the port industrial zone. Then the middle zone industrial area forms a small sector, to the south of which lies another second-class residential zone, followed by the wide area of first-class residential streets, schools with large grounds, and open spaces (Fig. 24). In the extreme southeast, a government sector can be identified. The pattern is indeed irregular, however, and is a highly generalized interpretation of the situation. The crucial arteries are Salim Road (which turns northward into Abdul Nasser Road), the western limit of Old Town, Jomo

Kenyatta Avenue, Kilindini Avenue, one of the arteries of the CBD, and Mnazi Moja Road.

Elements of a nucleated pattern can also be recognized, not only on the island itself, but in a view of the entire municipal area. As will be shown in the following chapter, the CBD fragments quite clearly into three individual zones, and in addition the arteries—

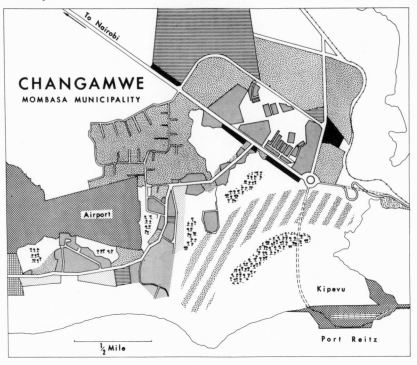

MAP 3

notably the northern section of Jomo Kenyatta Avenue—tend to serve as neighborhood shopping areas to crowded adjacent city blocks. But the municipality as a whole, including the mainland areas, displays considerable nucleation—which is not surprising in view of the tenuous connections with the island. Changamwe especially is developing core characteristics as a linear business area emerging along the main road to Nairobi (Map 3), but in Likoni also some retail establishments exist and their number is growing. The development of businesses has purposely been discouraged by Nyali Company, so that the northern mainland has a small commercial area just before the bridge is reached, at the intersection of the roads to Nyali and Freretown. As the proportion of Mombasa residents living on the mainland continues to grow, these embryonic core areas will develop into major outlying commercial zones.

THE MAINLAND AREAS

Since the consideration of individual functional zones of Mombasa will concentrate upon the contents of Mombasa Island, the outlying areas of the municipality should first be discussed. Of these, the area identified in census publications as the "West Mainland" is potentially the most important in terms of industrial development and population totals. In 1958 the Mombasa Municipality Census reported a total of 9,587 African residents in this northwestern area (as against over 11,000 on the northern mainland and 14,500 in the south), but since then, population has risen rapidly in Changamwe, the major unit located here.

In 1957, a municipal housing project was opened in Changamwe which was aimed at the reduction of poor housing, sanitation, and health standards in the area, but which in time came to be criticized for having contributed to substandard living itself. Rents were too high to attract people from the housing that was really in need of replacement, designs were not suitable for the circumstances of life, and some of the structures began to break down soon after they were put up. Located to the north of the Nairobi Road (Map 3), the housing estate has since been improved, but it does not match those constructed on the mainland (to which reference will be made later). In appearance many of the structures resemble the so-called "landies," consisting of elongated buildings containing as many as twenty adjacent rooms, each of which is rented out individually (Fig. 25).

Much of the Changamwe area still constitutes substandard housing, but signs of future improvement are already in evidence. The development of Port Reitz on this section of the mainland and the construction of a new access road to this area point to more jobs

FIGURE 25. The Changamwe housing development, established specifically for African residents by the colonial municipality during the
1950's, was not an unqualified success—partly because of the considerable distance from the island, the place of work for most of the potential
occupants. Shown here are some of the peculiar, elongated structures
containing rooms and apartments.

convenient to residential areas and increased municipal attention to
local problems.

The Mombasa-Nairobi road bisects Changamwe. To the west lies
the Port Reitz complex, including the municipal airport and a
nearby second-class residential area, which is owned largely by
Asians and is occupied by airport personnel. A peculiar mixture of
good and poor residences exists, the poor ones often occupied by
domestic servants who pay a low rent to whoever holds title to the
land on which the shelter has been built. The land fragmentation is
utterly irregular, a situation which the Changamwe project had
been designed to help combat. Few if any of the necessary facilities,
such as waste disposal and water supply, are available to the people
who must live in these mud and thatch dwellings.

A few light industries are making their appearance along the airport road, but the major industrial development (other than Port Reitz) on the west mainland, a large refinery, lies to the east of the Nairobi road. Here, too, lies Changamwe's rail connection with the interior. Commercial development along the Nairobi road until now has consisted only of a ribbon development with stores occasionally located along a side street (Fig. 26), and the only specialized business to be found in 1966 was a drive-in theater.

FIGURE 26. So irregular are the plots of land owned in Changamwe that a series of approximately parallel structures such as that shown above occurs only infrequently, and then only facing a major road. These particular buildings, one of them a duka-type shop, stand along the road leading northward from the Changamwe traffic circle shown on Map 3.

The area identified in the 1958 census as the "North Mainland" includes the estate of Nyali, the newly developing estate of Kisauni Point, and the settlements of Kisauni and Freretown (Map 4). At that time the population of this area was listed as 16,166, including 11,361 Africans, 3,192 Arabs, and 912 Europeans. During the past ten years Nyali has been developed considerably farther, and with the known rise in the African population the total for this

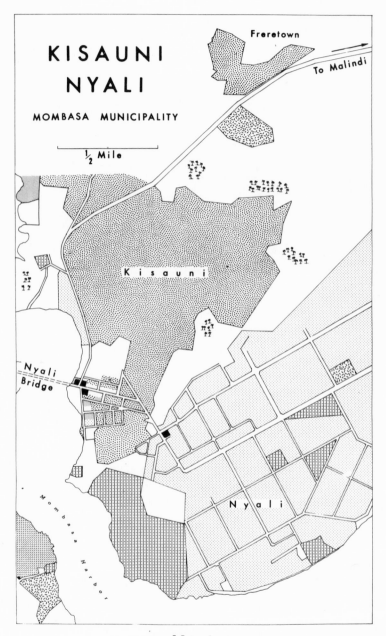

MAP 4

entire area today is probably near 25,000. Freretown is the historic settlement where freed slaves and their descendants found a place to live, while Kisauni is one of the most populous village-style suburbs of Mombasa, where gardens supplement the week's income, earned mostly on the island. The only industrial development of consequence is a cement factory, which employs several hundred people. Apart from the familiar haphazard pattern of land ownership and occupance, Kisauni has the disadvantage not only of distance to the island but also the toll to be paid at the bridge, which may appear to amount to little but, on a worker's wage, is a major expenditure. In addition, Kisauni has long suffered from a water problem.

The North Mainland presents a situation which requires a spatial solution. Here, a major first-class residential area adjoins a rural-type, third-class zone. In urban planning such a situation is normally avoided—a high-priced suburb is not likely to be constructed adjacent to an industrial region or near an existing area of deteriorated residences. In the case of Nyali-Kisauni, a belt of land separating the suburbs remains unoccupied and cleared, as a buffer between the two zones.

On the South Mainland, of which Likoni is a part, the 1958 census reported a population of 15,494, the great majority of it African (14,553). This area, still not connected by any permanent means to the island, is least effectively part of the municipality among the three mainland areas here considered. Only the eastern section of this area is represented on the map (Map 5), since the remainder consists of the familiar unplanned rural-type accommodations. For decades, the municipality paid little attention to this area, few roads were constructed, and services were nonexistent. Even when a high-class residential area was planned on the more favored coastal sites, little was done to render the area attractive to buyers. Not only was the ferry service inadequate, but there were no provisions for water supply, sewerage disposal, or electricity. Not surprisingly, by 1958 there were only 230 whites resident on the South Mainland, and even today the high-class residential zone of Likoni cannot compare to Nyali. Map 5 shows a planned road pattern; the actual roads of Likoni are still irregular dirt paths.

Recently a modest start was made to improve housing in the

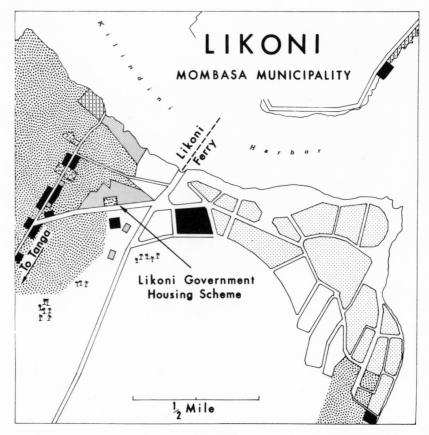

LIKONI

MOMBASA MUNICIPALITY

Likoni Government
Housing Scheme

½ Mile

MAP 5

presently third-class area at Likoni through the Ministry of Housing
of the Kenya Government (Figs. 27, 28). Still of modest size, this
project is designed to provide single-family houses with some yard
space rather than high-rise apartment space.

INDIVIDUAL FUNCTIONAL ZONES

Mombasa displays a core area, a rather incomplete middle zone,
a large set of residential districts, an industrial area, a transportation complex, and a government-administrative zone. While the
core area is the subject of Chapters 4 and 5, several of its characteristics are relevant here. The CBD shows several signs of immatu-

FIGURES 27, 28. The Likoni Housing Scheme, sponsored by the Ministry of Housing of the Kenya Government, will provide small houses for individual families rather than apartments such as those built on the island. This is one of the first attempts to improve the large southern part of the Mombasa Municipality. (A. Nazzaro)

rity: there are no department stores, many clothing stores do not specialize in men's or ladies' wear, and there is a large permanent resident population within the limits (later to be defined) of the region. Vertical development, as noted previously, is limited, but the district is of considerable extent. The size of the CBD is related to its elongation along Kenyatta and Kilindini Avenues and to its contiguity with the business-oriented Old Town.

While no continuous middle zone surrounds the CBD of Mombasa, those areas whose characteristics approach it most closely are the Old Town, to the east of the core, and the area of light industry to the west. The Old Town today is a maze of narrow streets and alleys with few of the facilities required for commerce, but a surprisingly large part of the zone is occupied by retail, wholesale, warehousing, and handcraft activities. The Old Town gives the impression of deterioration usually associated with middle zone areas, but this impression is somewhat exaggerated by the congestion and haphazard position of many of the structures. Some modernization has taken place on the foreshore (Fig. 29), but replacement of the

FIGURE 29. Modernization in Old Town: a new apartment building rises on the foreshore, overlooking old Mombasa Harbor.

old buildings in the town is a slow process which so far has made relatively little impact. For a sketch of a typical Old Town city block, see Map 7.

To the west of the commercial core lies the only area with true middle zone characteristics. Here are body shops, furniture makers, light metal works, and warehouses. There is some deterioration in the buildings, but the most serious problem appears to be the chronic congestion which prevails during business hours, when large quantities of goods are being loaded and unloaded without adequate handling facilities. The zone merges westward into the large transport-industrial complex, to which reference will be made later.

The residential areas of Mombasa present almost every conceivable variation existing in subsaharan Africa. To permit specifics as well as to facilitate generalization, a classification of residences has been adopted along very broad lines.[5] Easiest to identify are the first-class residences and residential areas. Largest and most prominent among these, of course, is the Nyali Estate on the North Mainland. There are only three others: Likoni an South Mainland, the Kizingo area, and Tudor. Reference has been made to Likoni and its slow development, but the two island areas remain. The Kizingo area extends from the area of government offices in the southeast, westward to the landing place of the Likoni Ferry. During the colonial period, this area was occupied primarily by government officials, administrative personnel, municipal officers, and others in similar capacities. Because of the nature of its occupants, Kizingo was never rigidly segregated, although it obviously was a dominantly European area. Today many houses here continue to be leased by the new government for the accommodation of its representatives.

The Tudor area in the northeast, however, was a distinctly and

---

5. The classification of residences used here is identical to that employed in previous studies. Factors considered include the state of repair of the dwelling, its age, the materials used in its construction (the use of corrugated iron sheeting for the roof normally labels a single-family residence as second class, thatch for the roof and mud for the walls, third class, etc.), as well as the size and quality of the garden and back yard, and the existence of servants' quarters, garage, and other outbuildings.

FIGURES 30–35. These photographs illustrate some of the contrasts in residential quality in Mombasa. Figs. 31 and 32 show first-class residences in Nyali and Kizingo, the latter overlooking the golf course and southern margins of the island. Second-class single-family residences are occupied by Asians (Fig. 32) and by Africans (Fig. 33), the latter in an officially sponsored housing scheme. Asian (private) and African (municipal) apartment houses are illustrated in Figs. 34 and 35.

Fig. 32

Fig. 33

FIG. 34

FIG. 35

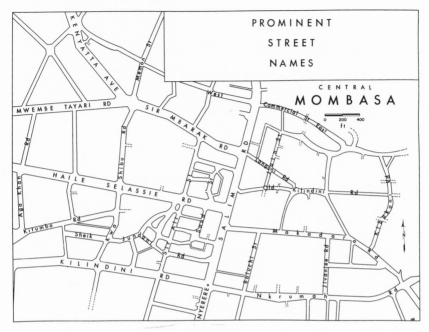

MAP 6

exclusively European zone. Land was owned by both whites and Asians, but the Asian landowners by agreement rented their properties only to whites. Tudor is still an exclusive area, and the peninsular part of the zone can be reached only by a single road (Map 2). The other part of this first-class area lies along the northern shore of the island, and here many Asians as well as whites own property. First-class residences in Mombasa are modern and spacious, and many have spectacular views of the coast (Figs. 30, 31). In the entire survey only one multiple-family building of first-class quality was encountered, and it was located in the Tudor area.

The second-class residential areas of Mombasa include the homes of a large section of the Asian population and several of the municipal housing projects in the city. A number of official agencies, for example the police and the government-run railways, have constructed housing for their employees, some of it of very good quality.

On the island, there are two major areas of such second-class housing. The first lies to the east of Jomo Kenyatta Avenue (Maps 2, 6) and includes both a large section of the Asian population as well as the high-rise municipal apartment houses designed for African occupance. The second area lies just to the south of Kilindini Avenue and adjoins Ganjoni Road. This is the major concentration in Mombasa of Goan residents. Few African families occupy single-family dwellings in this class, and those occupied by Asians, while often of good construction and considerable size, are commonly in bad repair (Fig. 32). The majority of people living in second-class accommodations reside in apartment houses. Even those single-story housing projects built by the government or municipality (Fig. 33) normally are row houses which accommodate more than one family under the same roof.

Much of the second-class housing of Mombasa is of the apartment variety. Privately owned apartment houses are usually in this class (Fig. 34), and the large and successful municipal scheme at Tudor has attracted many shantytown dwellers to better surroundings. In general terms the greatest impact made by these improvements lies in a semicircle which begins at Tudor, continues toward the Kenyatta-Salim intersection, passes through Kizingo, and terminates with the railway housing near Mbaraki Creek. This semicircle will be seen to lie on the side of the island away from the port and industrial facilities (Maps 2, 6), and as yet the least improvement has been made in the large residential areas between Kenyatta Avenue and this zone. The reasons are not difficult to enumerate: the eastern side of the island possesses more attractive residential sites, land prices are higher, fewer people in this area commute to the industrial area as distance increases. A glance at the land use map reveals that the third-class residential areas not only lie adjacent to the port and industries, but they occupy the very central section of the island—from all points of view the least desirable site for residential purposes.

The residences classified here as third class display a wide variation in quality, ranging from the most inadequate temporary shelters to sturdy, whitewashed structures. Mombasa's third-class areas are by no means all slums, and they are of great sociological significance. Here the correlation between race and quality of hous-ing, so commonplace elsewhere in colonial Africa for so long (first-second-third-class residences are occupied by whites-Asians-Afri-cans respectively) really breaks down, and even during the colonial period Mombasa never knew such strict segregation. Africans, Asians, and Arabs all live in these areas, sometimes sharing the same dwelling.

In Kisauni, Changamwe, and Likoni the vast majority of the people, in this case almost all Africans, continue to live in village-type surroundings, many cultivating a small *shamba* near their dwelling. But indigenous housebuilding has taken place on the island too, and while the product is not always adequate in terms of normal residential requirements, such housing has had a positive effect on the morale of the urbanized residents, for it has allowed a certain continued link with a known set of norms. These houses have been erected in a village layout of sorts, the grouping often reflecting the tribal background of the residents. Such indigenous housing is referred to as *majengos,* and the communities living here sometimes have their own shops, a church, and in a few cases a medical drugstore of sorts and occasionally even a school. The advantages of such communal living to the individual who enters the urban scene for the first time are obvious. He is able to rent a room here, share in activities, use the community services, continue to use his own language, and experience a more gradual transition than he otherwise might. Indeed, one of the disadvantages of the municipal housing scheme is that it has tended to destroy this social fabric, rendering the occupants more rootless and without a sense of belonging in any way to their new environment.

Despite the haphazard development of the majengo areas, the dirt streets, and the frequent congestion of the living quarters, few of these zones are actually slums. Considering the materials of which these suburbs are built and the limited facilities available to the occupants, streets are neat and people are comparatively well dressed and are carrying on one business or another (Figs. 36–41). In addition these areas possess the great merit of not being inevitably associated with one racial group. Perhaps one in four

FIG. 36

FIG. 37

FIGURES 36–41. Majengo-type dwellings in Mombasa exist over large areas: east of the port-industrial zone (Figs. 36, 37), north of the Old Town (Fig. 38, which also displays a local business area), and in a few scattered places elsewhere, including the area immediately south of the Tudor area. The population of these areas is racially mixed. Occasionally a temporary shelter makes its appearance (Fig. 41), but on the island, such structures are now rare.

FIG. 38

FIG. 39

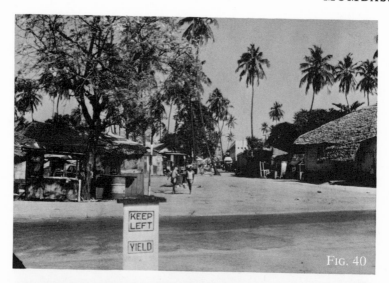

FIG. 40

FIG. 41

Asians, one in four Africans, and nearly half the Swahili residents of Mombasa Island live in majengo-type dwellings.[6]

This is not to suggest that indigenously made housing is never detrimental to an urban area. At times people entering the city have no ties, no immediate job, and no capital; they erect shelters such as that illustrated in Fig. 41, made from collected scrap material. Without any sanitation devices or the bare minimum of living space, these shacks, especially when they increase in number in a given area, are a danger signal to that part of the town.

Mombasa's industrial zone consists of several units, of which the southernmost lies south of Ganjoni along Mbaraki Creek. Mbaraki Creek was the first landing site in the modern development of Kilindini Harbor (a small jetty was built here before the turn of the century), and industrial development has existed here ever since. Today light industries are still located here, including a bottle factory and a beer brewery. The second industrial area was discussed previously, being in effect the western middle zone adjacent to the CBD. The third, and major, unit is the elongated zone which lies immediately adjacent to the port facilities (Map 2). This modern complex is the heart of Mombasa's industrial zone, and its well-planned and comparatively spacious area is served by a good railroad feeder system and a road network (Fig. 42). Automobile assembly, metal products (steel frames, aluminum products, metal containers), paints, insecticides, and other industries are located in this area. Other Mombasa industries include the manufacture of such consumer goods as soap, flour, matches, vegetable oils, various soft drinks, confectionery, and wood products. In addition, of course, there are outlying plants such as a brick factory at Changamwe and a cement factory on the shore of the North Mainland, opposite Mombasa Harbor. The majority of the heavy industries, though, are concentrated in the port complex (Figs. 42, 43).

The industrial and port areas draw thousands of workers, and the place of residence for most of these people is the third-class residential zone discussed above—the majengo area. As can be observed on the map (Map 2), the two zones lie adjacent to each other, and

6. G. Wilson, "Mombasa—A Modern Colonial Municipality," in A. Southall, *Social Change in Modern Africa* (London, 1961), p. 107.

FIGURE 42. The Mombasa industrial complex lies to the east of the port at *A*. The bluff is at *B*. Oil storage facilities lie in the foreground, with Kilindini Harbor at the right.

many laborers can quite conveniently walk to their place of employ. This process has been facilitated by the construction of several viaducts over the railway lines that separate the zones; the unoccupied area shown on the map is laced with many paths (Fig. 44).

There is a small sidelight to the subject of industrial areas which deserves mention. Visitors to the Tudor (African) residential development, which of course is not mapped as an industrial area, will become conscious of a soft chopping sound as they travel farther into this section of town. Eventually, if they allow their ears to guide them, they will come upon a most unusual sight—literally mountains of wood shavings, upon and within which stand some modest huts. These are the marks of the men who make some of the hundreds of wood carvings that abound on every East African market: their efforts are reflected by the scene shown in Fig. 45.

Nearly one-quarter of Mombasa Island is taken up by its impressive port and the developments related to it. This is the transporta-

FIGURE 43. Industries such as car and truck assembly plants are part of the industrial zone of Mombasa.

tion zone, including more than a mile of deepwater berths, a wide range of cargo handling equipment, miles of railroad tracks, a sizable petroleum storage facility, a cold store, coal berths, a lighterage wharf, and new developments at Port Reitz. If Mombasa has been the pulse of developing East Africa, Kilindini has been the pulse of Mombasa. Optimism and growth at Kilindini have always been closely paralleled by upward trends in population and city building elsewhere on the island. Symbolic of Mombasa's sprawl onto its adjacent mainland is the spread of port facilities at Kipevu, which also lies off the island. Each impetus at the port has been mirrored by growth in the city.

The development of Kilindini Harbor actually began before the turn of the century, and the first small quay was built in the late 1890's at Mbaraki, the southern inlet which was the first objective of port development. Nearby a lighterage wharf was built in 1907, and the establishment of the rail connection inland to Lake Magadi led to the building of another jetty, this time by a private company, in 1913. The real development of what is today the mile-long

FIGURE 44. Between the industrial area and the third-class residences adjacent to it is an empty belt, shown also on the map (Map 2). Many laborers can walk to work, as viaducts have been built to permit crossing of the railroad tracks. This photograph, taken from one of these viaducts, looks eastward into the middle zone of Mombasa and across the intervening empty strip. Thousands walk the paths on the left every day.

berth capacity of Kilindini began in 1921, when dredging for the first two berths began. The interwar period saw the construction of three more berths, the improvement of coal handling facilities at Mbaraki, and the beginning of a special petroleum wharf in the north. By 1958, the entire western margin of the island was occupied by port construction, and the need for additional facilities at Port Reitz had become obvious. Normally no month passes at Mombasa without delays for some of the vessels calling here.

In 1966, Mombasa possessed 13 deepwater berths totaling 7,690 feet, 10 transit sheds, and a 15-chamber cold store (Fig. 47). In addition two lighterage wharves were still operational, totaling 1,350 feet, with their 6 transit sheds, one cased oil wharf, 2 bulk oil jetties (tanker berths), a coal wharf, and a variety of

FIGURE 45. In North Tudor, wood carvers have been at work for so long that the shavings form veritable mountains—on top of which they continue to work at their lucrative trade. (A. Nazzaro)

buildings for baggage handling, customs, etc.[7] Of the four berths developed at Port Reitz, only the two nearest the island possessed sheds, while the others retained their open stacking areas (Figs. 47, 48). As shown by Fig. 48, Port Reitz still presents opportunities for further development.

One distinct functional zone remains to be identified, and it lies in the southeastern section of the island. This area was chosen by the British for the location of governmental buildings, and today a cluster of government and municipal offices is located here, including the treasury, court building, provincial administrative headquarters, the town hall, the regional assembly building, and the president's coastal residence. This clustering of administrative func-

7. *East African Railways and Harbours,* p. 56. In the same year, Dar es Salaam had only 3 deepwater berths, 2 transit sheds, one storage shed, and 4 lighterage wharves.

FIGURE 46.   An air view of Kilindini Harbor, showing the deepwater
berths, transit sheds, railroad emplacement, the bluff and industrial area
(right upper corner), and the oil storage area of Shimanzi. (Quality
Photo Process)

FIGURE 47. Port Reitz (foreground), with Kilindini Harbor, filled to capacity, in the background. The two sheds shown in the foreground are the only such facilities so far constructed at Port Reitz. To the left, off the photograph, is the Kipevu Causeway. The view is to the south.

tions is atypical of British-influenced colonial cities, since administrative buildings in other towns are often widely scattered throughout the urban area. Despite a certain concentration in Nairobi, for example, many offices lie far from Government House, and some are located in the outskirts. A situation similar to that of Mombasa was encountered in Dar es Salaam, where the German administration had contributed to a concentration of governmental buildings prior to the British occupation.

The land use map of Mombasa Island (Map 2) shows large areas to be devoted to schools and playgrounds, hospitals, cemeteries, and religious shrines. Indeed, at first glance this might strike the observer as the most remarkable feature of the urban pattern. It is without question an unusual phenomenon, and it is related to the multiracial character of the city's population—not merely the major

FIGURE 48. A southwestward view over Port Reitz, showing the open-air stacking area, two deepwater berths, and (at the right in the distance) tanker berth and pipeline. Port Reitz provides ample space for delayed vessels, and, as the photograph shows, considerable potential for future development.

racial divisions, but the fragmentation within each of these sectors. There are literally dozens of tribes, groups, communities, and families within each of the various large racial components of Mombasa's population, from the "twelve tribes" of the Arabs and the dozens of Asian families and communities to the more than eighty tribal African groups represented within the town. Of course not every one of these units is capable of establishing its own institutions, but many of them, through wealth, historical heritage, or by other means, have managed to do exactly that—from a modest mosque or a communal living house to wealthy schools, extensive cemeteries, and elaborate religious shrines. The situation is reflected by the wide distribution of this particular land use element. The map indicates that such areas are associated more closely with first- and second-class residential zones than third-class areas, but while their spatial impact may be less, all classes of residents, from the wealthy to the poor, possess such facilities.

In the functional structure of Mombasa, then, the significant features appear to be: first, the congestion marking certain island areas, especially in Old Town and in some of the majengo areas; second, the proximity of functional zones, that is, the close packing and occasional interdigitation of zones which under different circumstances would be separated; third, the attenuated nature of the central business area; fourth, the partial absence of the normal legacy of colonialism, namely the correlation between race and residential quality (though the housing developments described previously have tended to reduce racial mixing in residential living); fifth, the concentration of government functions in a distinct and circumscribed area; and sixth, the limited influence of the municipality in the rural-type suburbs that have developed on much of its mainland area.

Chapter 4 THE CENTRAL BUSINESS DISTRICT: DELIMITATION AND DIVISION

THE CENTRAL BUSINESS DISTRICT of Mombasa possesses several unusual characteristics. Most obvious is its arterial nature, not only along Kenyatta Avenue and Kilindini Road, but also northeastward along Abdul Nasser Road. Indeed, the only major artery passing through the CBD that does not carry retail functions with it as it emerges from the core is Nyerere Avenue to the south. (Map 6 provides all of the street names used in this chapter.) A second aspect of the district is the wide variety in shape and size of the city blocks upon which it has been built. Even the modern section of the region contains such narrow streets and alleys that it begins to resemble the Old Town into which it merges. The third peculiarity of the area relates to its margins. While the Old Town to the east

84

and the industrial-middle zone to the west form what might be viewed as normal transitions to other functional zones of the urban area, the CBD—especially in the north, but to some extent also in the Ganjoni area to the south—is literally invaded by residences. In previous studies, mention has been made of a salient aspect of East African cities—the large size of many city blocks and their hollow nature, that is, the existence of an empty interior which, in Lourenço Marques and Dar es Salaam, was often occupied by parking places, storage space, and, in a few cases, by workers' quarters. But the situation in Mombasa is such that virtually every available space, even inside CBD blocks, is used for residential living. This is obviously related to the crowding and congestion produced by the limitations of space on the island, but from the point of view of analysis of the functions of the CBD, it produces problems.

The situation is illustrated in Map 7. Based upon criteria employed by the municipality itself, these maps show the layout of several blocks within and just outside the CBD. The temporary buildings are those of the majengo type, illustrated in Chapter 3. Map *A* shows a block whose frontage is occupied almost entirely by retail functions, but whose interior space is used by several families who have constructed quarters there. This is not a particularly large block, as a glance at Map 2 will show, and the percentage of hollow space here is rather less than it is in many other city blocks within the CBD. The real invasion of majengo-type residences is displayed along the northern edge of the district, where the regularity of the block suggested by city maps is betrayed by a plan showing the nature of occupance (*B*). The frontage facing Commercial Street West is permanent and is occupied by retail establishments, and from this vantage point this appears to be a normal shopping street. But behind the strip of permanent buildings, the majority of the block is covered by third-class residential units (both temporary and semi-permanent buildings fall into the third-class category established in Chapter 3), which, it should be added, are placed here with a more-than-usual regularity. Map *C* represents a typical block of the Old Town. Even here, although there are more permanent buildings than in *B*, some majengos invade the interior parts of the

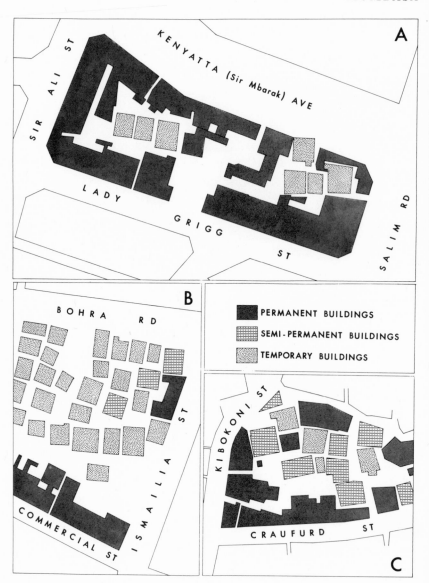

MAP 7

FIGURE 49. A southward view overlooking the southern part of Mombasa's CBD. In the left upper corner is the peak value intersection, on one corner of which stands the Catholic Cathedral. The north-south street in the left of the photograph is Salim Road, which at the intersection turns into Nyerere Avenue. The east-west street in the foreground is Haile Selassie Road, formerly Station Road. The modern buildings in the upper center face on Kilindini Road, and here are the most exclusive retail establishments in the city. (Quality Photo Process)

block. The need for the many walkways and alleys between buildings is obvious; population density here may exceed one hundred per acre.

The general situation is well illustrated by Fig. 49, which is a southward view overlooking the CBD. In the foreground, a city block faces on the main thoroughfare (Haile Selassie Road, formerly Station Road) linking the Old Town and modern CBD to the railroad station. Immediately behind the modern structures whose frontage is on Haile Selassie Road is a dense village of majengos, haphazardly positioned and walled off from the side street leading to the main thoroughfare.

These various aspects of the CBD render any analysis of its contents problematic—even more so than in the less arterial cores of Lourenço Marques and Dar es Salaam. In Lourenço Marques, the majengo problem does not present itself, and Dar es Salaam's CBD is a compact area whose boundaries are quite well defined. The CBD of Mombasa, however, tends to become more dispersed toward its borders, along some of which it interdigitates with non-CBD areas. But in other ways the three city cores resemble each other. All have a sizable permanent resident population within their limits, and upper floors are more often occupied by apartments than by offices. In 1960 Lourenço Marques, like Dar es Salaam, still retained an Old Town area similar in some ways to that of Mombasa, which functioned as a part of that city's CBD. Dar es Salaam's irregular street pattern resembles that of Mombasa (though Mombasa does not display the radials and traffic circles of Dar) and is likewise bedeviled by many narrow, alley-like streets incapable of adequately carrying even one-way traffic.

A reconnaissance view of Mombasa's core area quickly identifies the intersection of Kilindini and Salim (Nyerere) Roads as the peak value intersection, as reflected by the quality of retail establishments located here, as well as the type clustered in the immediate vicinity (Chapter 5). But as in the case of Dar es Salaam, pedestrian flows are heavier elsewhere. One contributing factor to this is the location, on one of the four corners of Kilindini/Salim, of the Catholic Cathedral, which effectively eliminates this southeastern block from contributing to the attraction of customers to this area. From the intersection (which lies on the margins rather than in the center of the CBD), Kilindini Road westward and Salim Road northward form the major business streets. The district extends almost a mile along Kilindini to the vicinity of the famed twin set of tusks arching across the six-lane avenue (Fig. 50). Salim Road is shorter, so that the hub of the CBD is in effect an L-shaped area. Here, no majengos interrupt the succession of retail establishments, and no ground floor space is used for offices. But beyond these two spacious streets, the character of the CBD changes a great deal, eastward into the Old Town and northwestward into the narrow side streets that mark much of the Modern downtown area (Figs. 51, 52).

FIGURE 50. A westward view along Kilindini Road, from the peak value intersection (left foreground) to the giant twin set of tusks, which are near the western limit of the CBD. The Catholic Cathedral is in the left lower corner (see Fig. 49 for a different view), and Salim Road runs north-south in the foreground. Haile Selassie Road is in the upper right corner. Note the limited vertical development, even here, in the hub of the district. (Quality Photo Process)

DELIMITATION OF THE CENTRAL BUSINESS DISTRICT

The characteristics described above render the delimitation of the CBD a difficult matter. The arterial nature of the commercial area is especially problematic: along Kilindini Road, for example, the highest quality establishments exist, but the floors above them and the space on the city blocks immediately behind them are often occupied by residences. This situation prevails along Kilindini as well as along Nkrumah, Nasser, and Kenyatta Roads; a sizable part of the CBD is of a ribbon variety. In addition, there are the problems usually associated with the delimitation of the CBD of colonial

FIGURES 51, 52. Aspects of the CBD of Mombasa. Wide, spacious Kilindini Road is flanked by impressive buildings near the peak value intersection (Fig. 51), while a few hundred feet to the north, a side street off Salim Road (Sheik Jundani Road) makes a very different impression (Fig. 52). Note the residential apartments above the stores.

African cities, problems which have been enumerated previously: the hollow nature of the blocks which in every other respect are clearly part of the zone, the absence of a reliable land value structure, the large amount of floor space devoted to non-commercial activities. As Map 7 shows, even when the frontage of a block is occupied almost entirely by retail establishments, these structures protrude into the inner part of the block for varying distances, so that the floor space available on any block cannot simply be calculated by the usual multiplication. The problem, which was first encountered in Lourenço Marques and subsequently again in Dar es Salaam, led to the development of a procedure to cope with it.[1]

The method is essentially quite simple, although its application in Mombasa produces some complications. It is based upon the degree to which available frontage has actually been occupied by CBD (particularly retail) functions. By frontage is meant the line of contact between the sidewalk and the buildings occupying city lots. Whether or not a block is fully occupied or has a hollow interior, its most immediate characteristics as a commercial unit are reflected by the nature of the establishments that are situated along this line. Across it steps every customer intent on doing business here, either in a ground-floor shop or in an upper-level office.

In order to determine the extent and limits of the CBD, then, two procedures are followed. First, the "percentage retail occupance" of each block in the core area is determined. This is done by calculating the total footage of retail frontage along any given block and dividing it by the total available frontage along that block. The figure arrived at is expressed as a percentage. Secondly, all individual retail establishments in the core area and in the adjacent middle zone and arterial sections are mapped, including banks and certain kinds of offices, such as those combining wholesale distribution with some retail selling and doctors' dispensaries which also sell drugs and medicines. The material gathered during the second step will be considered in Chapter 5. The retail frontage occupance arrived at is represented by Map 8.

---

1. The situation precludes the application of various standard methods of CBD delimitation, for instance that proposed by R. E. Murphy and J. E. Vance, Jr., "Delimiting the CBD," *Economic Geography,* XXX (1954), 189–222.

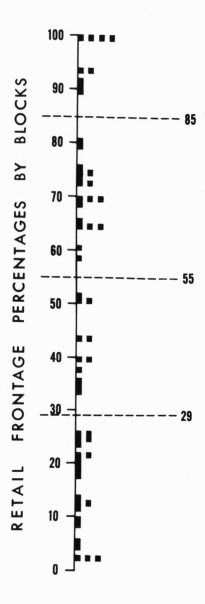

RETAIL INTENSITY DIVISIONS

Map 8

The frequency distribution of the percentages of retail occupance shows sizable breaks in several places. These breaks correlate remarkably with those found in Lourenço Marques and Dar es Salaam, the practice having been to determine those breaks nearest to the 25, 50, and 75 per cent level of occupance. The existence of such divisions at 29 and 85 per cent is immediately clear from Map 8, but at the 50 per cent level there is a choice—as, coincidently, there was in the case of Dar es Salaam. No clear choice emerges between these two breaks, which would lie around 55 and 47 per cent respectively, and elementary linkage analysis, while of course confirming the 29 and 85 per cent divisions, does not point to either. Since the higher of the two figures was taken as the dividing line in the previous studies, this was done again—with the added factor relating to the possibility of slightly inflated figures being taken into consideration. Hence the middle break lies at 55 per cent.

On the basis of these divisions, the core area was mapped as intensive retail frontage (86–100 per cent occupance), semi-intensive (56–85 per cent), extensive (30–55 per cent), and ultra-extensive (1–29 per cent). From the resulting map (Map 9), several aspects of the CBD emerge immediately. The first of these is the concentration of high-intensity retail occupance in two distinct areas: the Old Town and the "Modern" section of the CBD. Although wholesale establishments which combine some retail activity with their trade are common in Old Town, the high percentages of retail occupance by business enterprises on several Old Town blocks is a genuine reflection of the continuing importance of this area in the commercial life of the city. The other high-intensity area lies to the west of Salim Road and well to the north of the peak value intersection (P on Map 9). This situation is somewhat surprising after a reconnaissance of the CBD, for the heart of the district would appear to lie along the eastern portion of Kilindini Road and angle northward along Salim. But the blocks enclosed by Salim Road, Kenyatta (Sir Mbarak) Avenue, Sheik Jundani Road (to the south), and Sir Ali Road (to the west) generally contain retail establishments on all sides, whereas the blocks facing the southern side of Kilindini Road are occupied in this manner only

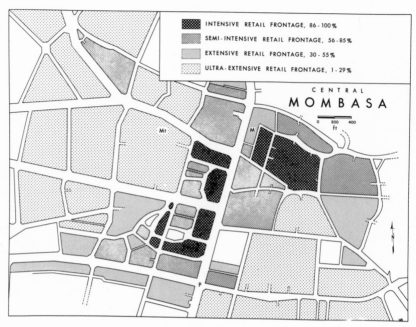

Map 9

along their northern frontage. Westward along Kilindini, this situation emphasizes the arterial nature of the district.

Another peculiarity of the commercial area is the high-intensity area lying north of the intersection between Kenyatta Avenue and Mwembe Tayari Road. Duka-type retail establishments increase in this area, which really lies in the heart of the majengo residential district. Again, this is an expression of the arterial character of the region. A somewhat similar situation prevails along north Salim Road and its extension, Abdul Nasser Road. Here, duka-type stores face the major avenue for nearly a mile north of the CBD, the buildings serving as both stores and residences. The extent of this arrangement is represented in Map 2, which also indicates the continuation of retail activities along North Kenyatta Avenue. In these areas, retail intensities are very low for obvious reasons, but the establishments which exist here nevertheless affect customer decisions—and thus influence establishments that are situated within the CBD. Hence, in the following chapter, stores lying along this artery and dealing in identifiable merchandise were included in the study of the internal characteristics of the CBD.

Unlike the commercial areas of Lourenço Marques and Dar es Salaam, therefore, Mombasa's CBD is not a compact area. Indeed, while the permanent market (*M* on Map 9) facing Salim Road lies well within the confines of the CBD, the day market (*Mt* on Map 9) is located in what is otherwise a low-intensity retail block. On a market day, the amount of commerce carried on in this area exceeds that in many a high-intensity block, but otherwise, this is an area dominated by residential apartments (Fig. 53). It is obviously impossible to compare temporary market stalls to permanent shop buildings, and the footage of the day market that happens to face on Kenyatta (Sir Mbarak) Avenue cannot be calculated as retail frontage. Nevertheless, this is a part of the city's commercial core, and in fact it forms a part of a market-type region which marks the entire northern section of the district.

This regional division of the CBD is represented by Map 10, which also shows the location of the boundary of Mombasa's commercial district as determined by the methods discussed above. The northern part of the CBD is identified as a "Market Region" which may be seen to overlap into the non-CBD block which contains the day market. Not only the day market and the permanent market on Salim Road but also two intervening blocks are included in this region. Here, as Chapter 5 will show, are concentrated many tailors, drapers, and other retailers whose shops give to Commercial Street West the narrow, alley-type appearance associated with markets everywhere, for they display their wares on tables or hanging from wires and ropes in front of their stores. No other part of the CBD resembles this particular area, and its location in the northern section of the commercial core may have some significance in relation to the residential zones and their distribution. To the northwest lies the major area of third-class residences, and Kenyatta Avenue is the artery that brings the vast majority of Africans into the commercial area to do business. Many Africans trade in the market and do not enter the CBD at all. Practically none come from the southern

FIGURE 53. Mombasa's open-air day market consists of numerous temporary stalls lined up crudely in a section of a city block facing Kenyatta (Sir Mbarak) Avenue. The majority of the permanent buildings on the block are apartment-type residential structures, and in these terms the block is one of low retail intensity. Nevertheless, it is an integral part of the city's commercial core. See also Map 2.

part of the island, where no third-class residential areas have existed. Hence those who do business in the market do not have to traverse the CBD to accomplish their goal.

There can be no doubt that the Market Region forms a rather rigid limit to the expansion of the CBD proper in this direction. The contrast between the set of high-intensity blocks discussed on page 85 and the adjacent market area is sharp, not only in terms of buildings but also from the point of view of customer type, goods traded, and prices asked. Here, one barters; in the CBD, one buys.

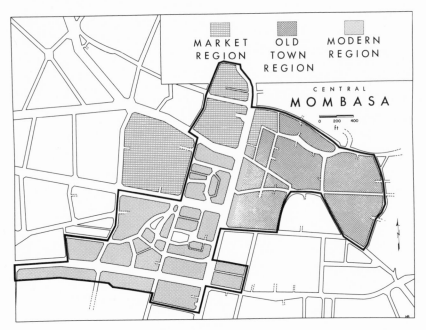

MAP 10

The second region shown on Map 10 is the "Old Town Region," some characteristics of which were identified on the preceding pages. Except for those Old Town blocks which face Salim Road, this is not a high-class commercial area; many establishments have no window displays but simply open their large wooden doors to the street for daytime activity. Wholesaling is a major occupation here, and there are many ground-floor offices. A considerable number of ground-floor residences also face on streets which are otherwise devoted to business enterprises. The Old Town is truly a mixture even today. On the somewhat schematic map, only the major streets of the area were used for calculation purposes. The detailed map (*C,* Map 7) of a town block suggests the maze of alleys that might have been used—but which would have rendered accuracy highly improbable.

The third section of the CBD to be identified is the so-called "Modern Region," which perhaps contains a good deal that is recent in construction but which is rather un-modern in appearance. This is the L-shaped area, which includes the peak value intersection and extends along Kilindini and south Salim Road, commonly viewed as the business center of Mombasa. Offices of major companies, banks, several hotels which have long catered to European demands, and high-priced curio and jewelry shops are located in this area. For the European shopper and the tourist, Kilindini Road remains the focus of the CBD, though pedestrian flow along Salim Road is somewhat greater and good-quality establishments are located there. The north side of Nkrumah Road displays comparable frontage, but the south side of this artery (formerly Fort Jesus Road) is occupied by the cathedral and a government building. Those establishments lying beyond are effectively outside the CBD.

The side streets between Haile Selassie and Kilindini, and between Salim and Sir Ali, present a very different picture. This is really the Asian part of the district, where shops are owned by Asians and cater to Asians; while many stores along Kilindini and Salim are also owned and operated by Asians, their appeal is rather to the European and visiting buyer. The distribution of retail establishments, considered in the following chapter, will underline this point.

The boundary of the CBD, also represented in Map 10, shows an attenuated area incorporating the three regions identified above. It is the line separating the three upper divisions of retail frontage intensity from the lower (ultra-extensive) division. Only the outlier along Kenyatta Avenue and the small triangular block in the southern part of the Old Town were excluded, the latter on the basis of limited contact with an adjacent CBD block and position of retail frontage. Although the area is contiguous and there are no island blocks of non-CBD characteristics within its boundary, the boundary does show the effect of the pull that has long been exerted in different directions: toward Kilindini with the rise of the new city, toward the Old Town and its continuing influence in the commercial life of the city, toward the north and northwest with the market-type activity prevailing there.

In Lourenço Marques and Dar es Salaam, the CBD also was found to be fragmented. In the Portuguese capital, there was a threefold division between an Old Town, a modern section, and a rather lower-class area. In Dar es Salaam, the racial divisions within the urban center as a whole seemed to be reflected by a fragmentation of the CBD, in which a "European" section and an "Asian" section emerged. It may be said that such division appears less prominent in the case of Mombasa, perhaps again mirroring the less conspicuous nature of racial contrast and segregation here. Nevertheless, as shown above, Mombasa's commercial core also does possess its own regions.

Chapter 5 INTERNAL CHARACTERISTICS OF THE CBD

THE CENTRAL BUSINESS DISTRICT of Mombasa, with its arterial extensions, is rather large for a city of this size, especially one that has evolved under British administration.[1] This impression is supported by the high total of retail establishments that exist in the commercial core, which is significantly greater (even allowing for Mombasa's larger population) than in the CBD of Dar es Salaam. Yet Mombasa's CBD shows many signs of immaturity. The lack of differentiation in the goods sold by certain stores is one example:

1. In Portuguese (and to a lesser extent, French and Belgian-influenced) African cities the CBD takes up a larger portion of the urban area, because of the tight packing of functional zones and the resultant limited area of the total urban region. British African cities have tended to sprawl (Bulawayo, Salisbury, Nairobi), and the CBD has normally comprised but a small part of the urban area.

clothing and shoe stores only occasionally sell gentlemen's or ladies' wear exclusively—usually both are sold. Even within the Modern region of the district many "general" stores remain (stores selling a variety of food and household goods). The large permanent resident population within the CBD is another sign: upper-floor apartments and even an occasional street-level residence still are found. Still another indicator is the absence of department stores, and perhaps this reflects the nature of the buyers who have frequented —and supported—Mombasa's commercial core. This city, like Dar es Salaam, has never had a large European (and wealthy) population. The white sector in both cities approached 5,000 shortly before independence; since then, permanent residents have declined in number. Neither Dar es Salaam nor Mombasa has had a department store, while Lourenço Marques, which in 1960 had over 30,000 whites out of only 110,000, had four such establishments.[2]

The objective of the present chapter is to determine whether the general functional characteristics of the city and the suggested regional divisions of the CBD are reflected by the distribution patterns of individual retail establishments within the commercial core. In both Lourenço Marques and Dar es Salaam such a correlation did emerge, but Mombasa, while racially even more heterogeneous than either of these two cities, has been more integrated. Even though the Old Town might be identified with Arab patronage and the Market region with that of Africans, the Modern region is not and was never as exclusive as Lourenço Marques' Avenida Republica or Dar's European region, perhaps. But if any such division has existed in practice in Mombasa, retail distributions are likely to reflect it.

The discussion which follows is based upon the increasing distances of the nodes of individual retail elements from the CBD retail node (Map 11). It should be emphasized, however, that *direction* is an equally significant indicator of the role of the particular element in the makeup of the CBD; reference will be made to

2. The use of Scott's method for the delimitation of the CBD is therefore precluded in Mombasa. See P. Scott, "The Australian CBD," *Economic Geography,* XXXV (1959), 259.

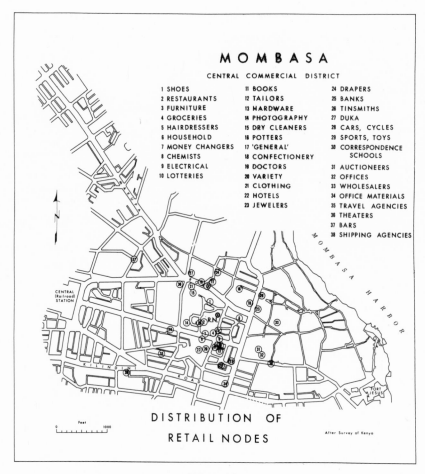

MOMBASA

CENTRAL COMMERCIAL DISTRICT

1 SHOES	11 BOOKS	24 DRAPERS
2 RESTAURANTS	12 TAILORS	25 BANKS
3 FURNITURE	13 HARDWARE	26 TINSMITHS
4 GROCERIES	14 PHOTOGRAPHY	27 DUKA
5 HAIRDRESSERS	15 DRY CLEANERS	28 CARS, CYCLES
6 HOUSEHOLD	16 POTTERS	29 SPORTS, TOYS
7 MONEY CHANGERS	17 'GENERAL'	30 CORRESPONDENCE
8 CHEMISTS	18 CONFECTIONERY	SCHOOLS
9 ELECTRICAL	19 DOCTORS	31 AUCTIONEERS
10 LOTTERIES	20 VARIETY	32 OFFICES
	21 CLOTHING	33 WHOLESALERS
	22 HOTELS	34 OFFICE MATERIALS
	23 JEWELERS	35 TRAVEL AGENCIES
		36 THEATERS
		37 BARS
		38 SHIPPING AGENCIES

DISTRIBUTION OF

RETAIL NODES

After Survey of Kenya

MAP 11

this aspect in the various cases to be discussed. Table 5 shows the sequence of retail nodes based on another criterion, namely, that of increasing distance from the peak value intersection. In order to assign the regional associations expressed in the table, proximity of the individual node to the nearest region was calculated, and for this purpose the actual borders of the market (rather than the entire low-intensity block upon which it lies, between Kenyatta Avenue and Selassie Road) were employed. It may be noted that such

TABLE 5

Sequence of Retail Nodes of Individual Functions Based on Increasing
Distance from Peak Value Intersection
(Regions Identified by Proximity)

Modern Region	Old Town Region	Market Region
34 Office Materials		
29 Sports, Toys		
25 Banks		
13 Hardware		
11 Books		
10 Lotteries		
20 Variety		
22 Hotels		
	32 Offices	
8 Chemists		
	36 Theaters	
	31 Auctioneers	
9 Electrical		
4 Groceries		
3 Furniture		
7 Money Changers		
5 Hairdressers		
2 Restaurants		
6 Household		
35 Travel Agencies		
14 Photography		
28 Cars, Cycles		
	33 Wholesalers	
		23 Jewelers
		18 Confectionery
		1 Shoes
		26 Tinsmiths
		16 Potters
		15 Dry Cleaners
38 Shipping Agencies		
		12 Tailors
		17 General
		21 Clothing
		19 Doctors
		30 Correspondence
		24 Drapers
		27 Duka
		37 Bars

functions as bookstores, banks, and travel agencies are distributed around a node lying within the Modern region, while wholesalers are concentrated upon the Old Town. Tailors, drapers, general stores, and duka-type establishments lie in the Market region, and significantly, the duka node lies farther than all but one of the other nodes from the peak value intersection. The table represents the beginning of a confirmation of the thesis stated above.

THE RETAIL ELEMENTS

Some of the problems involved in accurately mapping retail elements in an African CBD have been noted on previous occasions: the quality of the establishments varies greatly, as does their size; at times there may even be doubt regarding the items which bring the greatest revenues to the proprietor. The distribution of stores selling *shoes* (Map 12) is a case in point. As the map shows, these establishments are distributed throughout the CBD and its arterial extensions (the base map was drawn before name changes occurred, and Kenyatta Avenue is still identified as Makupa Road). In the vicinity of the peak value intersection, shoe stores may cater to either ladies or men, but such differentiation exists only in very few of the stores elsewhere in the district. Along lower Salim Road, shoe stores have large display windows and sell brand names imported from overseas; along Kenyatta Avenue the store may consist of a small room, without display facilities, which combines repair work with sales. The distribution of these shops is such that the resulting node lies nearer the CBD node than that of any other retail establishment represented in the commercial area. This is not surprising in view of the type of item sold.

Restaurants in Mombasa (Map 13) vary from high quality establishments to mere tearooms. Additionally, stores selling groceries and confectionery sometimes have facilities to permit people to consume food on the premises. Many of the restaurants in the Old Town and along Kenyatta (Makupa) Avenue are mere neighborhood snack bars, but along Kilindini and Salim Roads the appeal is to the businessman and the tourist. One hotel along Kilindini Road has a sizable porch-like arrangement for outside consumption of beverages and food, while others in the area advertise air conditioning, still a rarity in most of the district.

Several peculiarities relate to the distribution of *furniture* stores (Map 14). In both Lourenço Marques and Dar es Salaam, the retail node of these shops was positioned far from the CBD node.

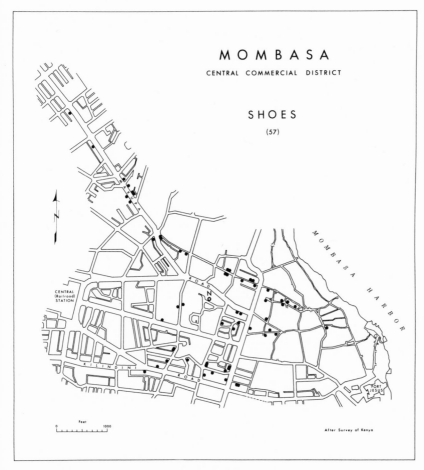

MOMBASA

CENTRAL COMMERCIAL DISTRICT

SHOES

(57)

MAP 12

Furniture stores normally require rather large premises, but they depend somewhat less upon display facilities. In Lourenço Marques, competition from department stores and other furniture stores in outlying parts of the city drove the furniture stores within the CBD into the lower class (and lower rent) area, where they occupied spacious accommodations. In Dar es Salaam, the retail node was also toward the lower quality part of the CBD, though some stores did occupy prime sites. Mombasa's furniture stores, on

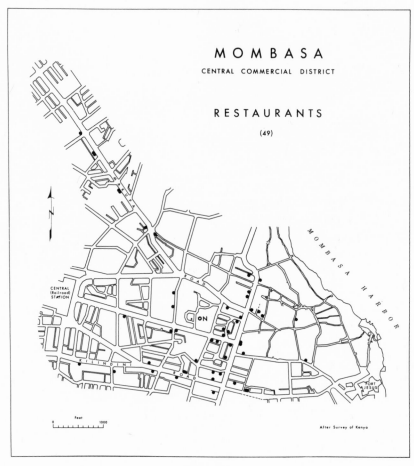

MOMBASA

CENTRAL COMMERCIAL DISTRICT

RESTAURANTS

(49)

MAP 13

the other hand, are generally smaller than those of Lourenço Marques or Dar es Salaam and are quite heavily concentrated in the Modern region of the CBD, immediately to the west of Salim Road. One reason for this distribution appears to lie in the nature of the merchandise sold: here furniture stores combine the sale of ordinary goods with that of decorative carved chests, copper ware, and the like; in effect they are partly curio shops. A situation somewhat analogous to that of Lourenço Marques exists along Nkrumah

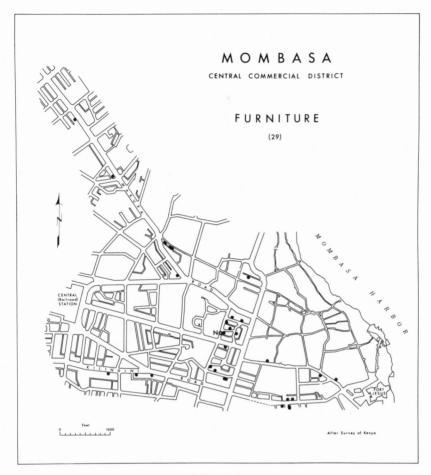

MAP 14

Road to the east and Kilindini Road to the west, where higher quality stores are located away from the highest rent section of the CBD but within walking distance from the hub.

A large number of *grocery* stores (Map 15) are heavily concentrated in the Modern and Market regions of the CBD, reflecting the patronage of Asian and African buyers. The heaviest concentration is immediately adjacent to the market off Salim Road, but other grocery stores occupy prime corner sites along the major avenues

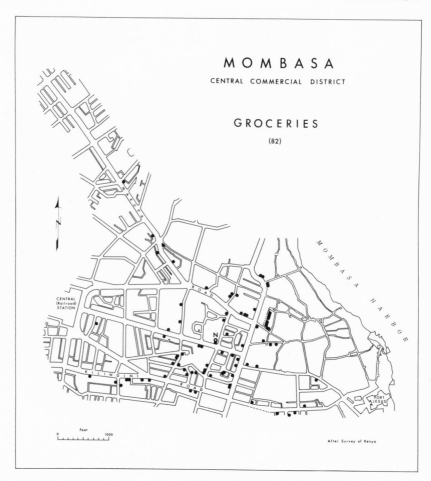

MAP 15

within the CBD (Fig. 54). The situation mirrors the diversity of tastes existing in the many communities of Mombasa and the sometimes particular requirements of the customers. The store illustrated in Fig. 54, for example, advertises not only its groceries but also its quality as a ship's chandler—the provider of essential supplies to the many coastal dhows and schooners that call at Mombasa Harbor every year.

Perhaps the term "food stores" should have been applied to the

FIGURE 54. Grocery stores in Mombasa often occupy prime sites on the major thoroughfares. The store illustrated here is located on Salim Road, and, as its signs indicate, deals in groceries as well as candles. It lies within a few hundred feet of the peak value intersection.

groceries of Mombasa, for many sell goods that would scarcely qualify as groceries. Some food, especially fruits and vegetables, is sometimes sold in the open air (Fig. 55), either at the municipal markets or at temporary stalls along the main thoroughfares.

Noteworthy in the distribution of groceries is their relative rareness along upper Kenyatta (Makupa) Avenue, especially in view of the large population concentrated adjacent to this artery and the obviously high daily requirements of this region. The answer appears to lie in the use of the day market by most African buyers, who would make up the largest potential patronage here. Hence the node for stores selling food lies to the south of the CBD retail node, while the majority of the consumers live to the north of the district.

Only three of the rather large number of *hairdressers* (Map 16) in the commercial area of Mombasa lie on or near the Kenyatta artery. The others mostly lie within the CBD proper, or along major streets nearby. Indeed, the establishments occupying good sites

FIGURE 55. A large open-air fruit stall on Salim Road. Such sales take place elsewhere within the CBD as well; opposite this particular establishment, in the median of four-lane Salim Road, is a similarly large open-air market of curios and souvenirs, especially wood carvings.

along Kilindini Road belie the normal pattern, which is that such shops are usually situated along side streets and in relatively poor locations, since they do not depend to a major degree upon pedestrian flow. The western location of the Kilindini hairdressers appears to be related to the port, from which sailors often walk toward the CBD along this major street. One noteworthy aspect of this retail function involves the ownership of the hairdressing establishment along the southern side of Haile Selassie Road. In 1963 this was the only shop owned and operated by an African proprietor within the boundaries of the CBD (Map 10). Hence, the social integration of Mombasa has not been mirrored by a similar situation in the core area. Here, the norm of commercial life in East Africa has prevailed.

Household stores (Map 17) exist in all three regions of the CBD, though only two of them occupy sites on major streets within the district. These stores sell kitchen utensils, ironing boards, and

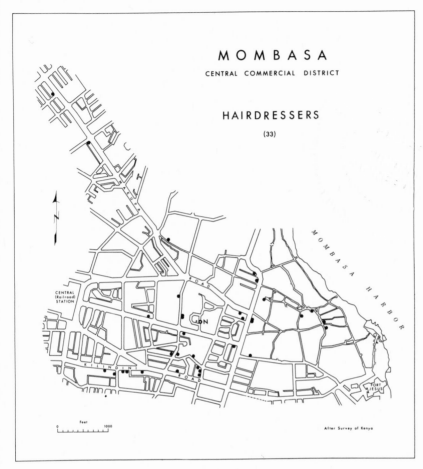

MAP 16

the like, but no electrical equipment or furniture. These are essentially low-priced establishments, and the distribution pattern with its concentration in the northern Old Town, along Commercial Street West and along side streets in the Modern region, reflects the need for cheaper sites and the patronage of the less wealthy buyer. Often such shops have no display facilities, and goods are set out in front of the building each shopping day.

Although Mombasa has several banks, a number of professional

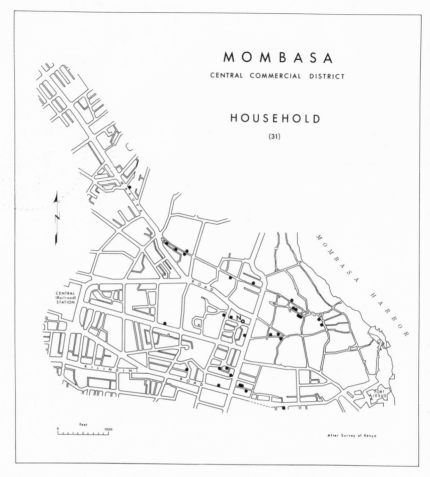

MAP 17

money changers manage to do business here. All of these (see Map
18) are located along major streets in the CBD or beyond: three
have their offices along Kilindini Road, another five are located
along Salim Road, and one operates on the Kenyatta (Makupa)
artery. Mombasa is the port of call for ships from many countries,
and sailors often desire to change coins (rather than notes), which
the banks will not take. Out of this trade the money changers are
able to make their profits, although they also attract business by

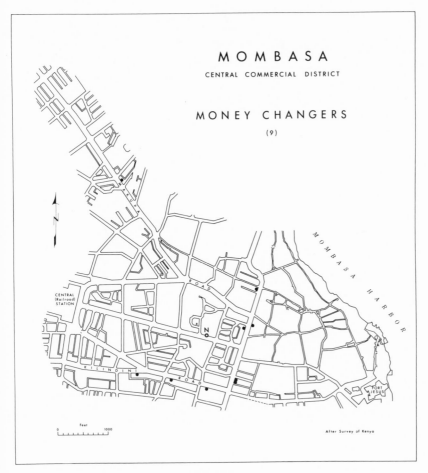

MAP 18

giving somewhat more favorable exchange rates than the regular *valuta* of some of the banks. As anyone with experience in these transactions will know, an added attraction of dealing with the money changers is the greater speed with which matters are handled; the delays at the major banks rank among the major sources of complaint on the part of tourists and visitors. Since independence, however, financial affairs have been regulated more tightly, and papers must now be shown for major dealings (even the cashing of

MAP 19

large amounts of traveler's checks). The money changers, therefore, are combining their activities with other transactions, including the sale of lottery tickets, newspapers, and magazines.

Two dozen *chemists* have their stores in the commercial area of
Mombasa, and all but five are located within the CBD proper (Map
19). Half of these shops are positioned on prime sites along Salim
and Kilindini Roads. This business clearly focuses upon the Modern
region of the CBD. Chemists sell medicines and handle prescrip-

tions; although chemists' shops are somewhat similar to American drugstores, they are far less diversified. They may occasionally sell cameras and film, but they practically never have a snack bar. Cosmetics may be carried, but not toys and stationery. The pharmacist who runs the store must be licensed, and commonly he and an assistant are the only persons operating the establishment. Hence medicinal items are the major items handled, and whatever else the store deals in is purely ancillary. Obviously chemists' shops are relatively complex businesses, and the few in Mombasa are long-term, permanent establishments.

Establishments dealing in *electrical* equipment of various kinds are numerous in the commercial core and by their distribution reveal a dependence upon pedestrian traffic and display (Map 20). Electrical stores are heavily concentrated in the Modern region of the CBD, but they exist also in Old Town and along Kenyatta (Makupa) Avenue. They deal mainly in radios and handle radio repairs, but record players, electric shavers, fans, air conditioners, and other equipment of this kind are also offered for sale. Both Dar es Salaam and Mombasa have a high number of these shops, reflecting the increasing wealth of the consumers in the urban area. While shopowners indicate that their largest patronage is Asian, they almost invariably report that African buyers are increasing in number.

A larger number of establishments dealing in *lotteries, pools,* and related betting activities was found than was anticipated (Map 21). Their number, four times greater than in Dar es Salaam, naturally reflects to some extent the fact that racing occurs in Nairobi; some of the betting is local. But these shops deal also in English Association Football coupons, the Irish Sweepstakes, and an array of other betting possibilities. The business is totally in Asian hands and is concentrated in the hub of the CBD, with only one or two exceptions. Kenya has opened a State Lottery, which should further benefit these enterprises, and the large tourist, transient, and ships' crew trade also are of significance.

Mombasa has no less than 34 stores selling *books and magazines,* and these businesses are distributed throughout the CBD (Map 22). This is nearly three times the number existing in Dar es Salaam

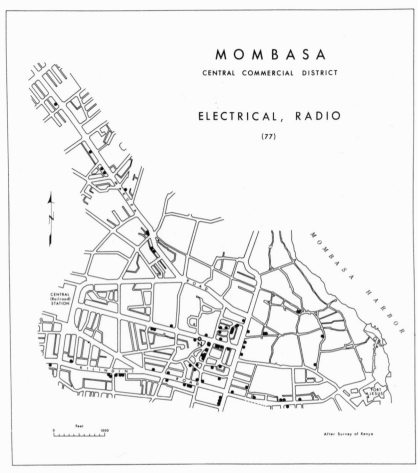

MAP 20

and no doubt reflects the inflated market created by the large number of visitors to the city. Many more major shipping lines call at Mombasa than at Dar es Salaam, and the tourist trade brings a larger number of guests to the city. Recently the airport at Malindi began to contribute to this volume, as economy flights from Europe landed there and tourists were transported by car to Mombasa (and on to Tsavo National Park). But the large number of bookstores also reflects the domestic situation. Mombasa has a very large

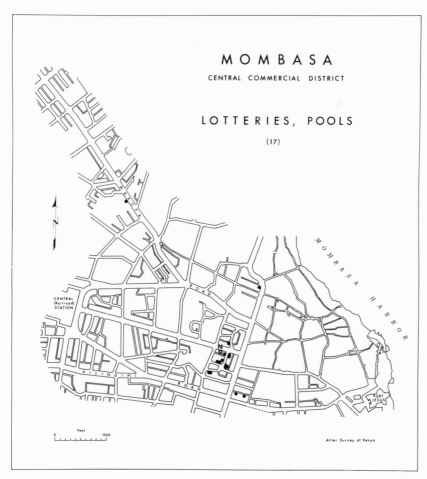

MOMBASA

CENTRAL COMMERCIAL DISTRICT

LOTTERIES, POOLS

(17)

MAP 21

school-going population, and many of the individual communities have their own schools and particular textbook requirements. Thus the institutional duplication referred to elsewhere has its effect in the CBD as well.

While some of the bookstores are located in prime sites and cater specifically to visitors, others have been accredited as official outlets for the schoolbooks used in the public schools. Still others are little more than magazine stalls. To the credit of the Kenyan administra-

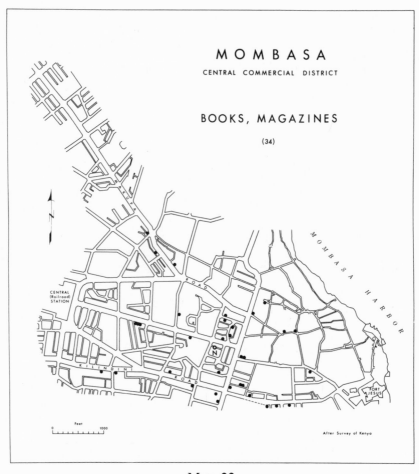

MAP 22

tion, practically every kind of material is available, from American magazines to Russian newspapers and even Chinese political propaganda.

There are over one hundred *tailors* in the commercial core of Mombasa, most of whom are located in the northern part of Old Town and along Kenyatta (Makupa) Avenue (Map 23). Indeed, the node for these establishments lies to the north even of the Market region of the CBD, reflecting the weight of the shops to the

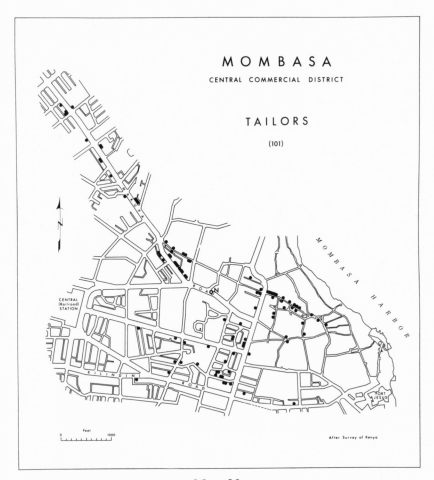

MAP 23

northwest. Tailors generally require little working space, and they often combine their living and working areas. Only a few of the tailors of Mombasa have display windows, and all of those are located in the Modern section of the CBD. A comparison between the present map and that of drapers (Map 35) and clothing stores (Map 32) reveals a linkage between these functions; tailors are often hired by clothing stores to make alterations or to do piece-work when staff is in short supply.

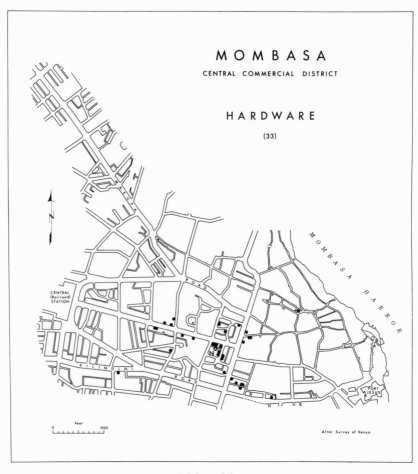

MAP 24

Stores selling *hardware* goods display a quite unexpected distribution (Map 24). Elsewhere these have been mapped with household stores, since it is often difficult to separate one from the other.
In Mombasa, almost all of the nearly three dozen hardware stores
are located in the Modern region of the CBD, while the household
stores mapped previously show a distribution throughout the three
regions of the district. The distribution may be a reflection of the
somewhat greater specialization of the goods sold by hardware

stores and the slightly higher prices these goods can demand. But it remains difficult to explain the total absence of these establishments along the entire length of Kenyatta Avenue and their almost complete absence from the otherwise varied Old Town.

The *photography* stores of Mombasa conform rather more to the expected pattern, for such specialty shops require capital, and, in the case of portrait work, skill. Nevertheless, some photography stores are located along Kenyatta (Makupa) Avenue, although the majority are positioned on good sites in the Modern section of the CBD (Map 25). There are no photography stores as such in the Old Town, although certain stores (some chemists' shops, for example) deal in cameras and film and thus constitute competition for these establishments. As a result, the node is drawn far to the west. Whether in the northwest or in the Modern region, no photography store is located on a poor site. All but four of these establishments are positioned on the major streets, reflecting their comparatively high quality.

Scattered throughout the commercial area is a surprisingly large number of *dry cleaners* (Map 26), remarkable because in 1962 not a single establishment in Dar es Salaam devoted itself primarily to this activity. Within the CBD proper, none of these shops occupies a prime site, but its patronage does not in any way depend upon window displays. Several dry cleaners are positioned along Kenyatta Avenue, near the large population concentrations flanking this artery. As a result, the node is drawn to the northwest. But even in the Old Town and in the Modern part of the CBD dry cleaners are established; the only part of the district to have no representation is the Market region—which, in view of the nature of business here, is to be expected.

Some commercial establishments in Mombasa are represented by less than a half dozen shops each, and since the node of the first of these, the *pottery makers,* places sixteenth in distance from the CBD node, these smaller business groups will be discussed here (Map 27). The four potters (represented by the solid circles on the map) are found in the Old Town and in the majengo fringes of the northern section of the commercial area. These locations place them near their customers, for the goods they produce are intended

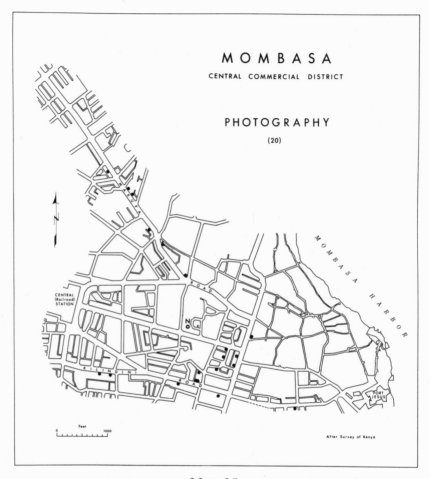

MAP 25

for use rather than ornamentation. Their small workshops are in fact minor industries, and the output and the turnover of their goods are impressive.

There are also four *tinsmiths* in the commercial area of Mombasa, and their art is the working of tin-coated iron, pure tin, and other metals. Only one tinsmith is located outside the Old Town, and the node, like that of the pottery makers, lies in the Market

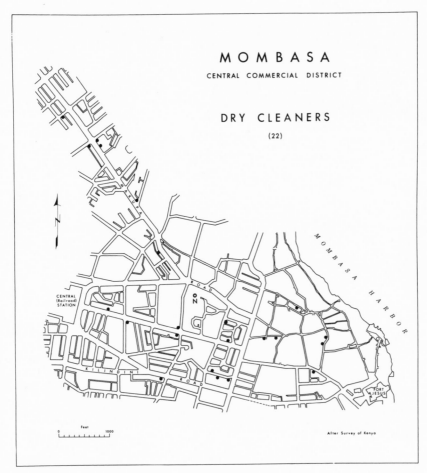

MAP 26

region (tinsmiths are represented by the open circles on Map 27).
Both activities depend upon the markets for the distribution and use
of their products, and they abound there. Tinsmiths also do a
profitable business in repair work.

Only five *bars* were found in or near the CBD (solid triangles,
Map 27), but this is no expression of the availability of liquor in the
district. Almost all establishments selling liquor do so along with

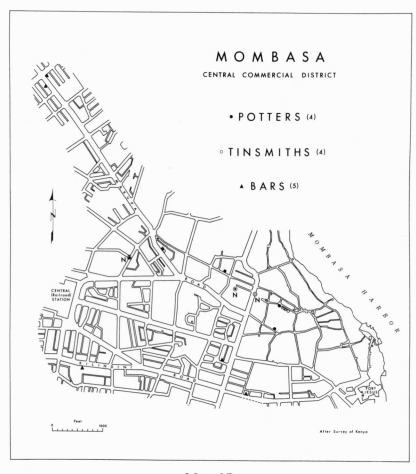

MOMBASA
CENTRAL COMMERCIAL DISTRICT

• POTTERS (4)

○ TINSMITHS (4)

▲ BARS (5)

After Survey of Kenya

MAP 27

the sale of other goods—food, entertainment (clubs), or accommodations. Indeed, there are very few pure and simple bars, and they
hardly constitute a factor in the retail structure of the CBD.

Like all other African cities, Mombasa has a large share of
so-called *general* stores, which sell an almost endless range of commodities. Some of these general stores, in the variety of their merchandise, begin to resemble department stores- -except that their
floor space is normally quite small and no opportunity for customer

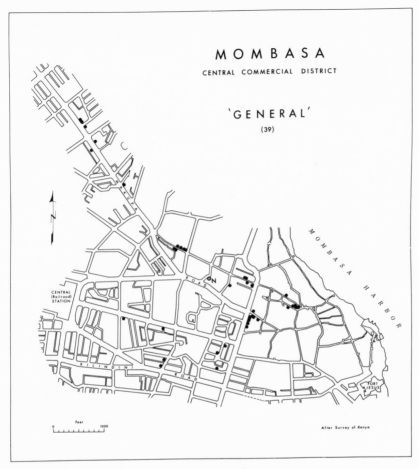

MAP 28

selection of goods can be provided for. Nevertheless, some general stores occupy rather good sites (Map 28), with frontage on Salim Road in the heart of the CBD. But most general stores are located in the Old Town and along Commercial Street East and West, occupying less favorable frontage. A few are positioned along North Kenyatta (Makupa) Avenue.

General stores (such as that illustrated in Fig. 56) may sell goods similar to those distributed by duka-type establishments, the

FIGURE 56. A large general store on Haile Selassie Road. Occupying a good site, this store sells a wide variety of goods and draws African and Asian (as well as Arab) patronage. To the left are several ground-floor offices (behind the closed doors); upper floors are used for residential purposes.

only difference lying in the quality of the building involved. The illustration shows a good, corner-site general store, rather large and, judging from the advertisements adjacent to the doors, carrying a wide variety of merchandise. Here one can obtain dried rice, kerosene, smoking needs, perhaps some clothing (shirts, shorts), canned foods, pots and pans, and more.

Mention has been made of the variety of tastes which result from the diversified communities that form Mombasa's population. In addition to the many grocery stores in the CBD, there are stores which sell so-called Indian *confectionery and spices* (Map 29). These establishments are strongly concentrated in and about the Market region of the CBD, though a few lie deeper into the Old Town and others are located along Kenyatta Avenue. This distribu-

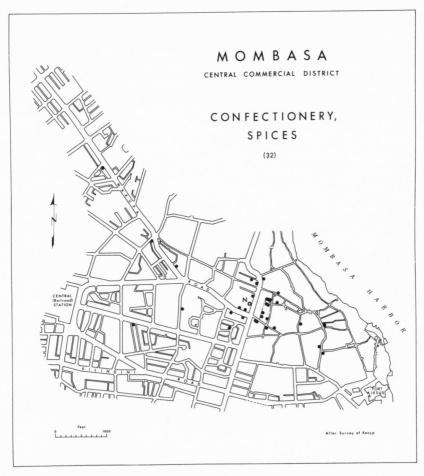

MAP 29

tion reflects the Asian patronage upon which these shops almost exclusively depend.

If a justification is necessary for the inclusion of *doctors' offices* (Map 30) in an appraisal of the retail structure of the CBD, a summary of the practices engaged in on these premises quickly provides it. Doctors' offices are more than medical dispensaries; medical treatment (mostly on a cash basis) is only one aspect of this busi-

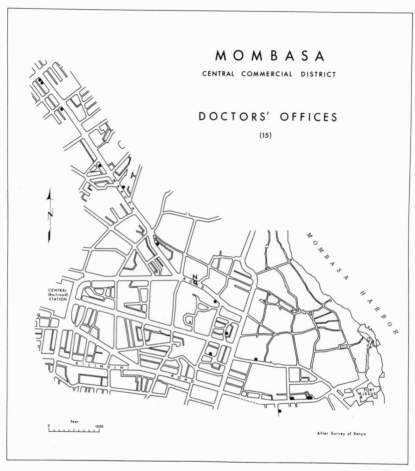

MAP 30

ness. Almost always drugs are sold as well, and sometimes equipment needed for convalescence is also available. The offices shown on the map are ground floor (street level) establishments of this kind, although there are many more doctors' offices situated within the CBD. A sample of the offices shown on the map, however, suggests that they are business operations like any other (hairdressers, for example); those along Kenyatta Avenue especially cater to the once-only customer.

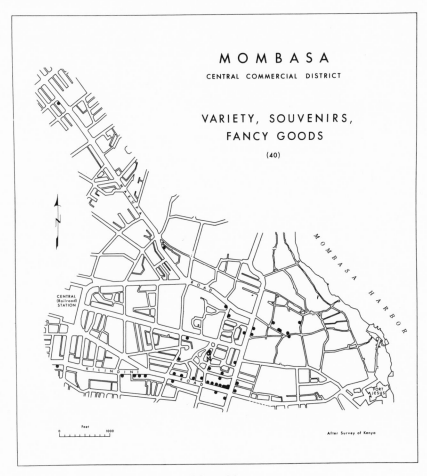

MAP 31

One of the most telling distribution patterns among the various retail establishments in Mombasa is that of *variety and souvenir* shops (Map 31). The majority of the forty stores are concentrated in the Modern region of the CBD; moreover, most of these are positioned along the most favorable artery for their trade, Kilindini Road. This lucrative trade is dependent upon exposure to pedestrian traffic, especially of tourists, and in no part of the CBD do visitors appear as frequently as they do on Kilindini Road near

Salim. The type and quality of goods sold in these establishments vary. Some stores aim at the market for trinkets, small carvings, postcards, cigaret lighters, and bracelets; others offer very select goods such as leopard skins, coats, hats, and purses, good African art pieces, and ornamental furniture such as carved Chinese chests and copper-tray tables. Whatever is sold, the profits are considerable and the stores manage to maintain prime sites.

A few souvenir stores have established themselves in the Old Town, in the vicinity of Old Kilindini Road. Most tourists enter the Old Town at one time or another, and shops here can afford to retail at somewhat lower prices than those along Kilindini Road and Salim Road. Only two stores—both along Kenyatta Avenue—appear to aim specifically at the local market through the sale of fancy goods suitable for gifts at local festivals and anniversaries.

A very different distribution is shown by a store type which caters largely to the domestic market: the *clothing* store (Map 32). While the node for such establishments lies to the northwest of the CBD node, clothing stores are distributed throughout the district, and some of them occupy excellent sites. Those positioned on Salim and Kilindini Roads are comparable to the best clothing stores anywhere, and this applies especially to the cluster around the peak value intersection. Here some stores do cater specifically to men or ladies, prices are very high, and imported brands are available.

Away from the major streets the quality changes. In the Old Town and along Kenyatta Avenue, clothing stores sell all kinds of wear, often combining this business with the sale of draperies; not infrequently some tailoring work is done on the premises as well. Second-hand goods appear, and the patronage reflects the contrast with the modern, large, wealthy establishments along Kilindini and Salim. In the far northwest there is actually a cluster of clothing stores serving the local area, which consists of a large third-class residential zone immediately to the west and second-class residential areas adjacent to the east. Hence the retail node has been pulled well to the northwest of the CBD.

No less than 14 *hotels* continue to operate in the commercial area of central Mombasa (Map 33). These range from mere rooming houses, with only rudimentary facilities, to such large and

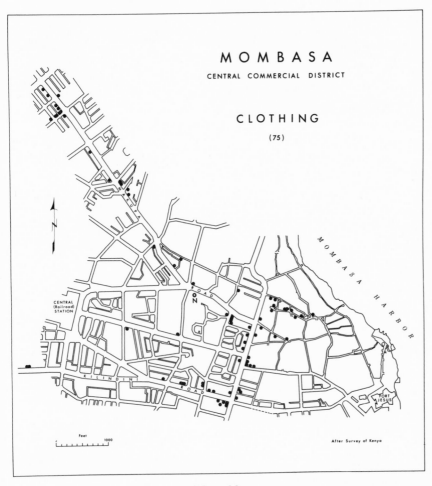

MAP 32

well-appointed establishments as the Palace on Kilindini Road. Traditionally, the location of a hotel has more or less determined the patronage it enjoys, and for decades the hotels have been largely segregated by race. This, of course, has broken down, but such establishments as those located on North Salim Road and those near the railroad station continue to serve almost exclusively the Asian, Arab, and African population. Wealthy non-whites do use the hotels in and near the hub of the CBD (Fig. 57), but the large

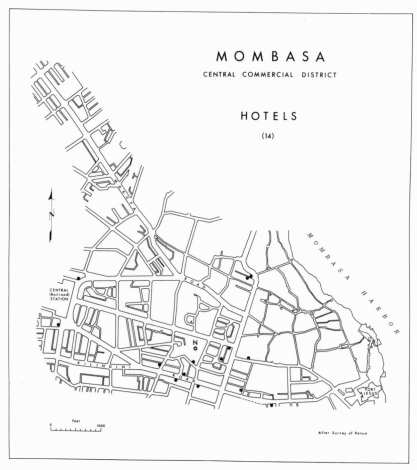

MAP 33

visiting and transient European population continues to make up most of the clientele here.

An astonishingly large number of *jewelers* have shops in central Mombasa, and a considerable number of these deal almost exclusively in watches (Map 34). Not only is the number extraordinarily large, but there is a strong concentration in the Old Town, while the Modern region of the CBD has merely a normal representation of this function.

FIGURE 57. The hub of the CBD is a crowded area, with parking at a premium and rush-hour congestion a daily occurrence. Shown here is the New Coastal Hotel (since renamed the Central) at the Haile Selassie-Salim intersection on the right, a new garage and gasoline station on the left. The frontage in the background is on Salim Road; the view is toward the southeast.

From the distribution pattern and the concentration on the sale of watches it is possible to understand the causes of this situation. To a large extent, the Old Town remains the major market for the crews of coastal vessels and dhows that journey to the Arab world. To these sailors the availability of watches presents an opportunity to increase their income, for in the course of their travels they will reach ports located in countries where the sale of watches and related items is restricted, or was within recent times: such countries are India and Indonesia. Here, a profit of several hundred per cent may be made on a watch bought in Mombasa, and so the trade in these items has steadily increased. It is not surprising, then, to see so many jewelers in the city, nor is it difficult to understand why so large a number of them deal almost exclusively in watches. The concentration of jewelers in the Old Town naturally reflects the

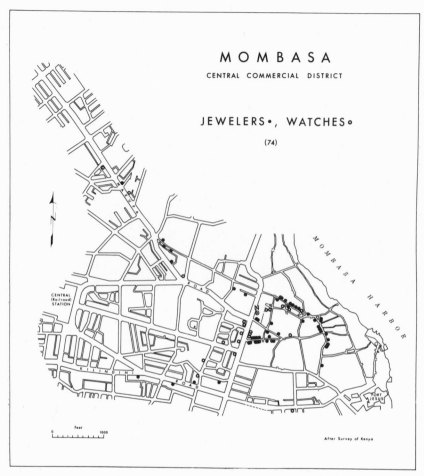

MAP 34

source of the patronage. Of course, there are other factors at work: premises in the Old Town are cheaper, and Arabs as well as Asians share in this trade. But the major element is the inflated market created by conditions elsewhere—and Mombasa's connections with the outside world serve it well.

So heavy is the concentration in the Old Town that the node of these establishments lies to the east of Salim Road, one of the few businesses to be positioned there. The jewelers in the Modern region of the CBD are mostly located, as would be expected, on prime sites along Kilindini and Salim Roads. From the point of view of exposure to both markets (the local as well as the overseas visitors), Salim Road would seem to be the most advantageous artery for jewelry stores, and, indeed, every jewelry store along Salim concentrates on dealing in watches.

Almost one hundred *drapery* stores exist in downtown Mombasa, and, as might be expected from the nature of this business, there is an exceptionally heavy concentration of these establishments along Commercial Road West, in the Market region of the CBD. In Lourenço Marques these stores are located mostly in the Old Town, and in Dar es Salaam, successions of drapery stores occupy entire block frontages, a situation which obviously parallels the one in Mombasa (Map 35).

A few drapers maintain stores on Salim Road and West Kilindini Road, and this serves to emphasize that, as in the case of clothing stores, there is great variation in the type and quality of the shops involved. The cloth sold in the Market area is geared to the bulk of the consumers, who are mostly Asian, while the higher priced and often imported materials sold in the Modern region of the CBD appeal to the wealthier customers. As a glance at the mode of dress of the Asian and Arab populations shows, the turnover in these goods is considerable.

The *banks* of Mombasa's commercial area mostly lie along Kilindini-Nkrumah Road (Map 36). Asian, Arab, and European banks are represented here by branches: the Bank of Baroda, Bank of India, Habib Bank, Ottoman Bank, Barclays, Standard, National and Grindlays, and the Netherlands Bank have offices here. Mombasa has a financial district, in effect, along Nkrumah Road, where most of the major banks are located, but a few branches are positioned along West Kilindini Road and North Kenyatta Avenue. There is ample justification for including banks in a discussion of the retail structure of the commercial core, for their influence on the commercial life of the city is considerable: by offering savings facilities they attract the patronage of all sectors and communities, and by making available loans to businessmen, they permit the building of stores and the start of new ventures.

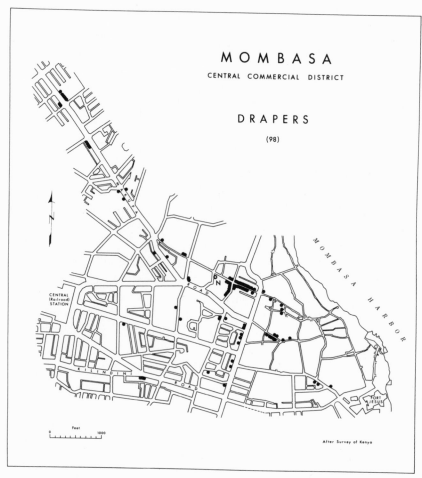

MAP 35

Many *duka-type* stores remain in Mombasa, even in the Modern region of the CBD (Map 37). The duka-type store sells a variety of goods somewhat similar to that available in the general store, though the range is usually less and the premises are of poorer quality. The duka store not only exists in every East African community, from the largest city to the smallest village, but the Asian has carried this type of economy into the interior as well. The survival of so many duka-type stores in downtown Mombasa is an

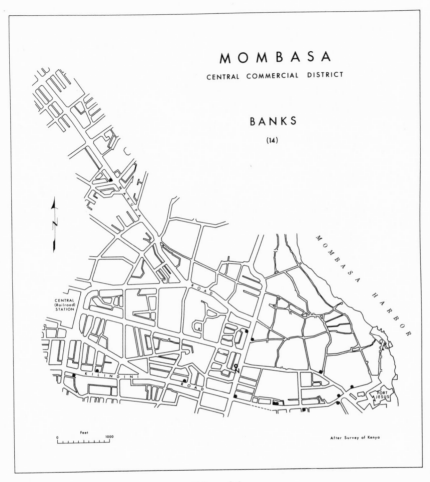

MAP 36

unusual aspect of the city, for in Dar es Salaam no such situation presented itself. This is obviously a function of the nature of separation which was instituted in Dar es Salaam during the colonial period, when a wide, empty belt of land was retained between the built-up portion of the central city and the nearest majengo-type residential area. No interdigitation such as exists in Mombasa was permitted. Mombasa, on the other hand, displays a transition between the CBD and the adjacent (northern) residential zones, and

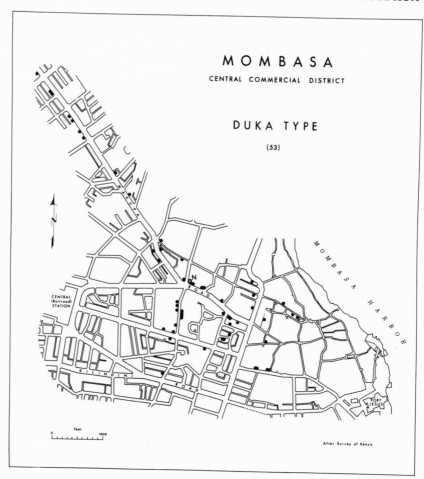

MAP 37

as a result city blocks in the downtown area are occupied not only by residences of the majengo type (as discussed in Chapter 3), but also by duka-type stores, the commercial equivalent of the majengo.

While many of the duka stores lie to the west and northwest of the CBD proper, in 1963 others still were situated on quite good sites on Station Road (Haile Selassie Road) and North Salim Road. A few remain in the Old Town, and there is a cluster along Kwa

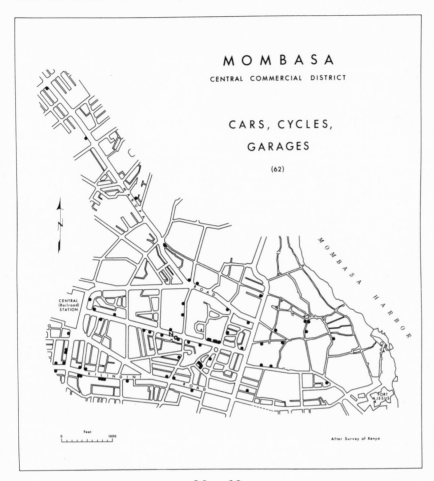

MOMBASA

CENTRAL COMMERCIAL DISTRICT

CARS, CYCLES,

GARAGES

(62)

MAP 38

Shibu Road, along the northern part of which the node for these establishments is located.

Distributed throughout all parts of the CBD, and reflecting the increasing mobility of the population as well as its increasing income, stores selling *cars and cycles* and *garages* servicing them are large in number (Map 38). Many of these lie immediately to the west of the CBD boundary, along Haile Selassie Road and West

Kilindini Road, but surprisingly few are positioned along Jomo Kenyatta Avenue (Makupa Road), the major exit from the city into Kenya. The goods sold by these establishments are imported, of course, and they are bulky; hence the westward location of many of these stores may reflect the convenience of proximity to the port and industrial area. Indeed, some of those located along West Kilindini Road are within the middle zone of the small industry flanking the commercial area.

Only seven stores in downtown Mombasa deal specifically in *sporting goods and toys*. Such stores depend upon the varied pursuits of wealthier people, and there are comparatively few of these in Mombasa. The majority of the population, the Africans, basically play one sport, namely soccer, for which only minimal equipment is needed. The Europeans brought the variety of sports activities to which the Western world is accustomed: in addition to soccer, they introduced golf, cricket, hockey, handball, boating and fishing, and other forms of relaxation. But their numbers were never very large, and their requirements remained limited. Some Asians have taken up various English sports, especially cricket and hockey, and the schools teach these, but comparatively few residents of Mombasa practice sports for which much equipment is needed.

Not surprisingly, the shops selling these goods are distributed almost exclusively through the Modern region of the CBD; one store lies in the Old Town along Old Kilindini Road (very near Salim), and another is located along Nkrumah Road (Map 39). The node is among the nearest to the peak value intersection, although the sites occupied are not always the best in the area.

A large percentage of the people resident in Mombasa remain illiterate, although now virtually all youngsters go to private or public schools, and many older people, too, want to learn to read and write. To serve this market there are *correspondence schools,* which dispense lessons in writing in much the same way that a shopkeeper sells his goods. Some of these correspondence schools are one-man operations, though others are more permanent institutions of some size with a staff of several persons. Only one such school (Map 40) is located on one of the major streets within the CBD, while the others are on lesser sites and along Northwest

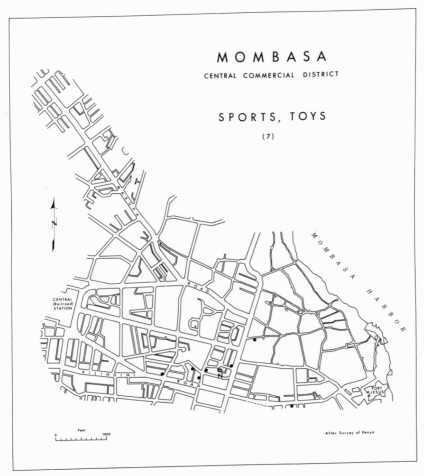

MOMBASA

CENTRAL COMMERCIAL DISTRICT

S P O R T S ,   T O Y S

(7)

MAP 39

Kenyatta Avenue. The location of the node suggests the source of the majority of the patronage for these establishments, which remain among the more unusual aspects of this city.

The node for *auctioneers* lies well within the Old Town (Map 41), though the establishments lie mostly about the fringe of this region. These stores did an especially good business during the period of the decline of Arab influence and power, when many once-wealthy families were forced to give up much of what they

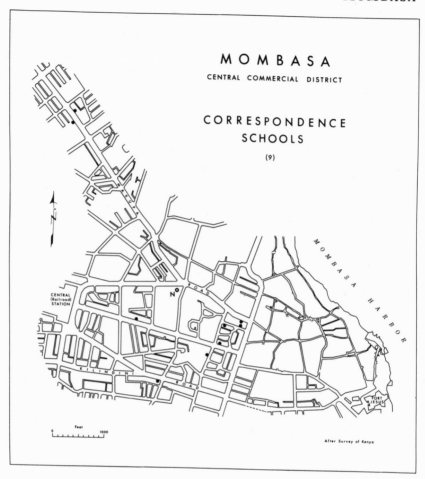

MAP 40

owned. Still today there is sufficient turnover to keep several of them in operation: departing Europeans have recently contributed to their profits. Some auctioneers' shops are at the same time pawn-shops, and there are always wares on hand for inspection or direct sale. Still, none of them occupies a prime site, and less than half their total lies within the boundaries of the CBD.

The existence of street-level *offices* throughout the business area of Mombasa has been mentioned previously. Their distribution is

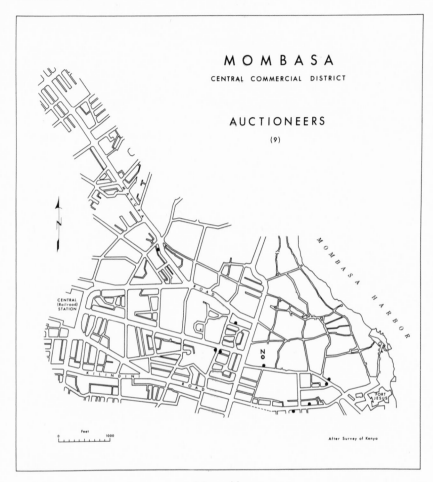

MOMBASA

CENTRAL COMMERCIAL DISTRICT

AUCTIONEERS

(9)

MAP 41

represented by Map 42, which shows that these establishments lie in the Old Town and in the Modern section of the CBD, but not in the Market region. No offices of this kind lie along Kenyatta Avenue.

The offices here included are those of lawyers, insurance agencies, employment agencies, and the like; doctors' offices and the establishments of wholesalers are not represented on the map, as they constitute other categories. This aspect of the CBD of Mombasa resembles a similar situation in Dar es Salaam, where the task

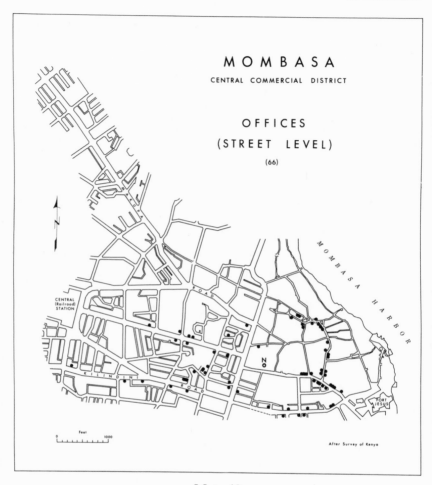

MAP 42

of identifying the offices of doctors, wholesalers, and others proved insurmountable. The present type of office is located on premises which often resemble a store; there may be a window display, and many establishments give some evidence of prosperity, judging from the office equipment in use and the sites occupied. A considerable number lie in the Modern region of the CBD, some along Kilindini Road.

By contrast, the establishments of *wholesalers* are very heavily

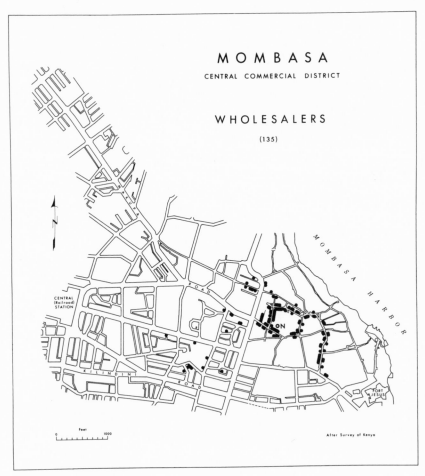

MOMBASA

CENTRAL COMMERCIAL DISTRICT

WHOLESALERS

(135)

MAP 43

concentrated in the Old Town, and their node lies far to the east of that of the CBD as a whole; well over 100 of the 135 wholesalers mapped had their offices east of Salim Road (Map 43). This, of course, reflects the degree to which this business is in Asian hands. Many wholesalers combine the retail sale of some of the goods they distribute with their shipping function, and so it is sometimes difficult to distinguish the wholesaler from the retailer, especially in the look-alike premises of the Old Town. Almost without exception

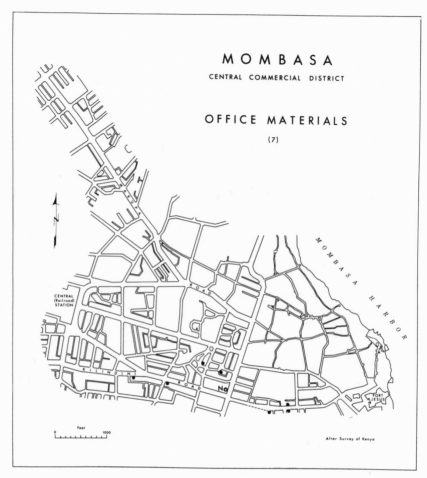

MAP 44

these are the shops whose big wooden doors open to the street to reveal a host of packed and stacked goods, while a desk and some file cabinets constitute the office. The merchandise is distributed by handcart and truck, and the area has a market-like appearance on any business day.

Stores selling *office materials* and equipment are located in the Modern part of the CBD (Map 44), and of the seven existing, five lie along the Kilindini-Nkrumah artery. This is obviously a high-

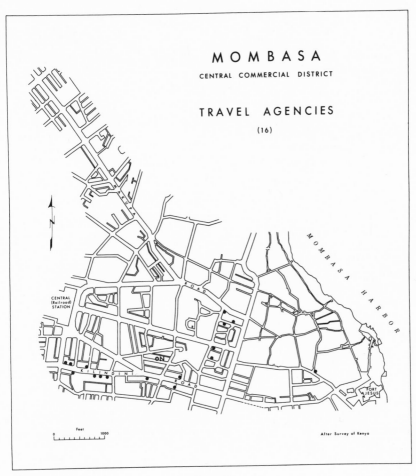

MAP 45

priced specialty business, and thus, while the retail node lies far from the CBD node, it is closer than any other to the peak value intersection. Despite the fact that the CBD of Mombasa in every way is larger than that of Dar es Salaam, there is only one more of these establishments here than in the Tanzanian capital.

A cluster of *travel agencies* lies along West Kilindini Road, near the port but in effect outside the CBD (Map 45). This western area, which draws the node for these establishments in that direction, is also the site of the city's information bureau, offices of the Automobile Association, and other businesses related to travel. With the ever-increasing mobility of the population, the number of travel agents in Mombasa is no surprise, but their distribution is another matter. Most tourists and visitors are likely to look for the travel agent's services along East Kilindini Road, where only two such offices are located. None existed along Salim Road at the time of mapping, although a few were positioned in side streets off Salim and Kenyatta (Sir Mbarak).

If the westward concentration of travel agents is port-related, it reflects the high volume of sea traffic by passengers traveling to and from India and Europe. The major shipping lines (such as Union Castle) have long called here, and many Asians have taken visits to their original homeland. By comparison, air traffic to Mombasa has only recently begun to make a major contribution to the tourist flow. The peak period for total passenger flow (embarkation as well as disembarkation) in recent years was during the late 1950's and early 1960's, when many Europeans left Kenya, mostly by sea: nearly 10,000 in 1961; 15,000 in 1962; 13,000 in 1963; 11,000 in 1964; and a little more than 8,000 in 1965.[3] In 1960, Mombasa's port processed 83,500 passengers; in 1964, over 70,000; and in 1965, nearly 63,000.[4] But the number of disembarking passengers is rising while that of those embarking is declining, which indicates that the number of visits by tourists is growing, while the flood of emigration may be abating. In the total figures, however, the Asian contribution figures significantly: from 1955 to 1959, an average of 10,000 annually arrived for purposes of permanent immigration, while from 1960 to 1965, annual emigration totaled over 4,000, mostly by sea.

The four major *theaters* of downtown Mombasa are all located to the east of Salim Road, two of them well inside the Old Town (Map 46). The main theatergoing population appears to be Asian, and Asian films are shown exclusively by some theaters here and else-

3. East African Statistical Department, *Economic and Statistical Review*, no. 18 (March, 1966), p. 10.
4. *East African Railways and Harbours*, p. 63.

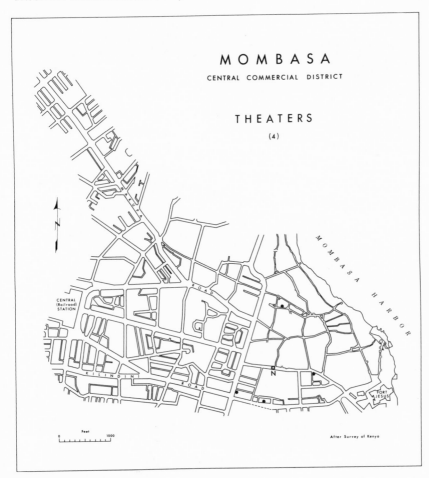

MAP 46

where in the city, while others alternate British and American films with Asian pictures.

The distribution of *shipping agencies* also reflects the westward location of the port (Map 47), as most of these establishments are positioned on far West Kilindini Road, well outside the CBD. In both Lourenço Marques and Dar es Salaam, the advantage of proximity to the harbor was reflected by a similar location of ship-

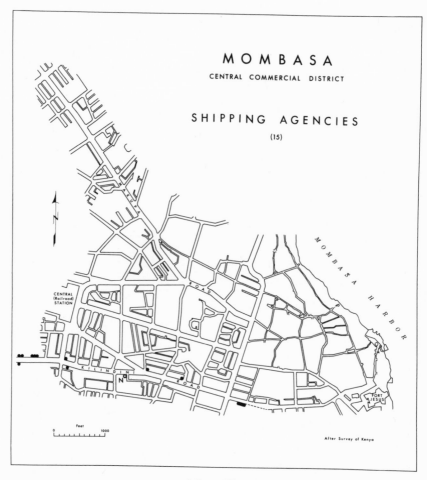

MAP 47

ping agencies, and in the case of Mombasa, the degree to which the
Old Town has lost its former importance as a portuary service area
is underscored by the concentration of these offices away from this
zone.

The CBD of Mombasa, then, displays a regional division which
appears to be based upon economic and functional criteria primarily, rather than on mainly racial foundations. While certain stores,
such as those of the duka type, are drawn in the direction of the

residential zones from which they attract the majority of their customers, these residential zones are themselves racially mixed: such
stores are patronized by Africans, Asians, and Arabs. Whereas
some stores (such as the Indian confectionery shops) cater specifically to the tastes or demands of one particular community in
Mombasa, these stores do not form part of an exclusively Asian
district in the CBD. No real European and non-European divisions
seem to exist in the district, at least not to the degree that they have
existed in other colonial cities; while most whites would tend to
shop along the Kilindini and Salim thoroughfares, they are outnum-
bered even there by shoppers of other races. Again, the Market
region in the northern section of the commercial core is by no
means entirely an African area of business: Arabs and Asians, as
well as Africans, operate and patronize the stalls and shops. The
sequence of retail nodes with increasing distance from the peak
value intersection represents a rather normal, expected, economi-
cally-based succession, and in no way does it mirror a sharp racial
fragmentation of the CBD, as was the case in Dar es Salaam.

The size, in terms of the total number of establishments, of
Mombasa's CBD is somewhat inflated by the growing tourist trade
and the number of crews from visiting ships. Here the commercial
core reflects the volume of port traffic in some very distinct ways.
Normally, the proportion between Dar es Salaam and Mombasa, in
terms of the number of stores oriented to the local market, is
approximately what would be expected on the basis of population
totals: Mombasa has between 10 and 20 per cent more establishments of certain types (clothing, shoes) than the Tanzanian capital.
But while Dar es Salaam has a mere 38 jewelers, Mombasa has
approximately double that number. There are many more variety
and souvenir shops and stores selling ornamental furniture. A
glance at the number of ships, their size, and the disembarking
passenger totals for Dar es Salaam and Mombasa suggests the
measure of Mombasa's lead in this area. In the number of ships,
Mombasa in 1965 led by a margin of 3 to 2, and the number of
visiting passengers at Mombasa was twice that of those disembarking at Dar es Salaam. The benefits to the commercial core are
obvious, and they are reflected in many tangible ways.

Chapter 6 CONCLUSIONS

MOMBASA RESEMBLES ITS COUNTERPARTS in East Africa in several ways. The over-all residential pattern reveals the elements of racial segregation which were characteristic of every colonial city during the period of European hegemony. As in other East African cities the vast majority of small businesses are owned and operated by Asians. Here too, most of the urban area was planned and laid out during the past 75 years, though the rate of growth of the city increased markedly after the Second World War, when various colonial development projects were completed and development in the hinterland was stimulated.

On the other hand, a set of unusual conditions and circumstances has combined to produce a city which, in East Africa, is in many

152

FIGURE 58. This air view shows dramatically the contrasts between the urban landscape prevailing in the Old Town (foreground) and the southern and southwestern parts of Mombasa Island. The small jetties of old Mombasa Harbor can be seen at the foot of the Old Town, and some coastal schooners are in port. At left is Fort Jesus, while the modern section of the CBD can be seen at the right. The entrance to Kilindini Harbor is in the distance, with Likoni beyond. (Quality Photo Process)

ways unique. The shift of focus of commercial activity from the eastern part of the island westward permitted the survival of a thousand-year heritage in the Old Town, with its unmistakable spatial and architectural characteristics (Fig. 58). The continuing role of this area as a part of the commercial core of the city was illustrated by the distribution patterns of various retail establishments in the central business district. Despite the relative inaccessibility of the Old Town and its poor facilities for business, hundreds of shops continue to compete successfully in this location.

The marked heterogeneity of Mombasa's population is another contributor to the city's singular character. Not only are there sizable Asian, Arab, and white minorities, but Somalis, Seychelles, and Chinese add to the almost infinite variety of people in this truly cosmopolitan town. The African majority itself is fragmented into dozens of tribal communities and their social organizations, while the religious and familial division within each of the minority groups has left its marks upon the urban landscape. The racial segregation that might have developed here with a strictness and intensity equal to that of other colonial cities never materialized to the same degree; but for the various modes of dress, it would be difficult to distinguish many of the groups represented here from one another. Cases in point are the Africans and the Swahili Arabs, and the Hindu, Moslem, and Christian Asians.

If European rule did bring a certain racial separation it did so in a more permissive way than almost anywhere else in British East and Southern Africa. Of course the price of land and large residences placed most first-class homes out of the reach of both Africans and the majority of Asians, but nonwhites did own land and property in Kizingo prior to independence, and even the exclusive "European" area of Tudor was partly owned by Asians—and segregated by private arrangement rather than law. But all races used the buses, post offices and municipal facilities were always open to all, and few "Europeans Only" signs were ever seen in this town.

However, even if the correlation between race and residential quality (discussed in Chapter 3) were a fact in Mombasa, the urban pattern would still be one of interdigitation and close proximity. The limitations of space on the island have rendered the luxury of sector-type separation (as in Dar es Salaam and Port Elizabeth) prohibitive, and virtually everywhere—Nyali-Kisauni is an exception—residential zones of different classes closely adjoin each other. Anomalously the municipal administration, by sponsoring various apartment projects, unintentionally helped intensify racial separation. These projects were always aimed at the reduction of substandard housing on the island, but by allotting apartments to families on the basis of need and in order of application they tended to remove Africans randomly not only from the often closely-knit majengo communities in which they lived, but from their Asian and Arab neighbors there. When racial tensions occasionally increased,

FIGURE 59. The new Mombasa: a part of the municipal housing project at Changamwe on the mainland. Here lies the city's greatest challenge—to improve living conditions and bring services to its far-flung suburbs.

as they inevitably must in a community as varied as this, some observers blamed the new apartment projects for contributing to them.

Mombasa's great challenge lies on the mainland, where the impact of the municipality as a beneficial agent is just beginning to be felt (Fig. 59). Apart from the private residential estates that exist here, only Changamwe has been notably affected by the services and improvements municipal government must bring; Kisauni and Likoni have yet to be seriously involved. This is not altogether surprising, for Changamwe (the west mainland) has most to offer. Here, Port Reitz is developing, and a major refinery has been built. The main road to Nairobi and the only railroad linking Mombasa with its hinterland pass through Changamwe. An increasing number of laborers cross the Makupa Causeway each business day to reach their jobs on the island. Thus Changamwe is the first of the mainland areas to begin developing an urban environment, and the

FIGURE 60.   Mombasa has only begun to reap the tourist harvest. With its breeze-cooled climate, its incomparable beaches, nearby Shimba Hills and Tsavo National Park—not to mention its own historic attractions— one might prophesy a bright future for the tourist industry. The city already boasts several excellent hotels, including the one illustrated here, which underscore the growing confidence in tourism as a source of revenue.

administration of the municipality has concentrated its first efforts off the island in this area. But in effect the municipality has barely begun to implement its plans for the 90 per cent of its territory that lies on the mainland, and the costs are heavy.

Nevertheless, the future is bright for this city, the first port in East Africa, the second largest industrial complex in this vast, developing region. Its site, unlike that of Dar es Salaam, its major competitor, presents no serious obstacles to a continuation of the development that has marked recent decades. Mombasa should share in the profitable tourist trade which Kenya is strongly encouraging (Fig. 60); in short, there is a great deal of potential in several spheres.

Mombasa never displayed the excesses of colonial rule, the sharpness of segregation, or the harsh inflexibility that led to intense conflicts elsewhere. But independence will bring changes here as it did in Dar es Salaam, where the impact of Africanization was felt severely and immediately and was soon reflected in the urban landscape: the German-built government complex on the foreshore was quickly torn down to make way for modern buildings. The new policies of Kenya, too, will bring change to Mombasa. If the commercial life of East Africa has long been dominated by Asians, in Mombasa it has not only been dominated but controlled. But now, many Asians who are non-citizens face insecurity and uncertainty; many are unwilling to make investments needed to keep their businesses healthy. The order to commercial establishments and industries that a larger percentage of Africans must be employed has affected the make-up of the labor force in Mombasa's CBD quite considerably. Whether the new situation will eventually lead to empty storefronts and a decline in the prosperity of the CBD, as some businessmen predict, remains to be seen. What has been written here represents essentially the situation at the time of transition; in the future it may provide a useful basis for comparison.

BIBLIOGRAPHY

As STATED IN CHAPTER 1, the geographical literature—and, indeed, that in the related sciences—on Mombasa is very limited. Among the books listed below, only some historical works focus specifically upon the city; the others contain useful information on the town as part of a broader context. However, no attempt has been made to collect indiscriminately all materials relevant to the Coast in general. The definitive geographical treatise remains I. S. van Dongen's "Mombasa in the Land and Sea Exchanges of East Africa," *Erdkunde,* 1963. A great deal of information is contained in G. M. Wilson's *Mombasa Social Survey,* a typewritten document available for inspection at the Vice President's Office, Nairobi. Several base maps of the urban area can be obtained. The Survey of Kenya in October, 1963 published a multicolored map of Mombasa Island (scale 1:14,000) which is remarkable in its accuracy and wealth

158

of detail. Base maps of the central business district, though somewhat outdated, are available at 1:10,000 (four sheets, including much of the mainland), and parts of the downtown area have been mapped at 1:600. The former are available in Nairobi only, the latter in Mombasa at the Lands and Survey Office. Air photographs also may be obtained, and the area was flown twice in recent years, in 1957 and 1963, though at different heights. The two sets of maps yield valuable insights, especially with regard to the mainland sprawl and its progress.

BOOKS

AXELSON, E. *South-East Africa, 1488–1530.* London, 1940.
————. *South-East Africa, 1600–1700.* Johannesburg, 1960.
BADGER, G. P. *History of the Imams and Seyyids of Oman.* London, 1871.
BELLINGHAM, B. L. *Mombasa: Guide to Mombasa and Surroundings.* Mombasa, n.d.
BOXER, C. R., and C. DE AZEVEDO. *Fort Jesus and the Portuguese in Mombasa, 1593–1729.* London, 1960.
BRADY, C. T. *Commerce and Conquest in East Africa.* Salem, 1950.
BROWN, A. G. *Year Book and Guide to East Africa.* London, 1951.
BURTON, R. F. *Zanzibar, City, Island, and Coast.* 2 vols. London, 1872.
CHURCH, A. *East Africa: a New Dominion.* London, 1927.
COUPLAND, R. *East Africa and Its Invaders.* London, 1938.
————. *The Exploitation of East Africa, 1856–1890.* London, 1939.
DELF, G. *Asians in East Africa.* Oxford, 1963.
DUNDAS, C. *African Cross Roads.* London, 1955.
DUYVENDAK, J. J. L. *China's Discovery of Africa.* London, 1949.
ELIOT, C. *The East Africa Protectorate.* London, 1905.
FITZGERALD, W. W. *Travels in the Coastlands of British East Africa and the Islands of Zanzibar and Pemba.* London, 1897.
FREEMAN-GRENVILLE, G. S. P. *The East African Coast: Select Documents from the First to the Early Nineteenth Century.* Oxford, 1962.
————. *The Medieval History of the Coast of Tanganyika.* London, 1962.
GRAY, J. M. *The British in Mombasa, 1824–1826.* London, 1957.
————. *Early Portuguese Missionaries in East Africa.* London, 1958.
HAMILTON, G. *Princes of Zinj.* London, 1898.
HILL, M. F. *Permanent Way.* 2 vols. Nairobi, 1951–1959.

HINAWY (HANAWY), M. A. *Al-Akida and Fort Jesus, Mombasa.* London, 1950.

HOBLEY, C. W. *Kenya from Chartered Company to Crown Colony.* London, 1929.

HOLLINGSWORTH, L. W. *A Short History of the East Coast of Africa.* London, 1959.

HOURANI, G. F. *Arab Seafaring in the Indian Ocean in Ancient and Early Medieval Times.* Princeton, 1951.

International Bank for Reconstruction & Development. *The Economic Development of Kenya.* Baltimore, 1963.

INGHAM, K. *A History of East Africa.* London, 1962.

JOELSON, F. S. (ed.). *Eastern Africa Today and Tomorrow.* London, 1934.

KIRKMAN, J. S. *Gedi: a Palace.* The Hague, 1963.

———. *Guide to Fort Jesus Mombasa.* Mombasa, 1960.

———. *Men and Monuments of the East African Coast.* London, 1964.

MARSH, Z. *East Africa through Contemporary Records.* Cambridge, 1961.

MEINTZERHAGEN, R. *Kenya Diary, 1902–1906.* Edinburgh, 1957.

MORGAN, W. T. W., and N. M. SHAFFER. *Population of Kenya: Density and Distribution.* London, 1966.

OLIVER, R., and G. MATHEW (eds.). *History of East Africa.* 2 vols. Oxford, 1963.

OWEN, W. F. W. *Narrative of the Voyages to Explore the Shores of Africa, Arabia, and Madagascar.* 2 vols. London, 1833.

PERHAM, M., and M. BULL. *East Africa, November 1889 to December 1890,* Vol. I of *The Diaries of Lord Lugard.* Evanston, 1959.

PRINS, A. H. J. *Sailing from Lamu: a Study of Maritime Culture in Islamic East Africa.* Assen, 1965.

———. *The Swahili-Speaking Peoples of Zanzibar and the East African Coast.* London, 1961.

REUSCH, R. *The History of East Africa.* New York, 1961.

RUSSELL, C. E. B. (ed.). *General Rigby, Zanzibar, and the Slave Trade.* London, 1935.

STIGAND, C. H. *The Land of Zinj, Being an Account of British East Africa, Its Ancient History and Present Inhabitants.* London, 1913.

STRANDES, J. *The Portuguese Period in East Africa.* Nairobi, 1961.

TRIMINGHAM, J. S. *Islam in East Africa.* London, 1964.

VAN DONGEN, I. S. *The British East African Transport Complex.* Chicago, 1954.

VILLERS, A. *Sons of Sinbad*. London, 1940.
WILSON, G. M. *Mombasa Social Survey*. Nairobi, 1957.

ARTICLES

CHITTICK, H. N. "The Shirazi Colonization of East Africa," *Journal of African History,* VI (1965).
————. "Kilwa and the Arab Settlement of the East African Coast," *Journal of African History,* IV (1963).
EMERY, R. N. "A Short Account of Mombasa and the Neighboring Coast of Africa," *Journal of the Royal Geographical Society,* III (1854).
ETHERINGTON, D. M. "Projected Changes in Urban and Rural Population in Kenya and the Implications for Development Policy," *East African Economic Review,* I (1965).
FREEMAN-GRENVILLE, G. S. P. "Swahili Literature and the History and Archaeology of the East African Coast," *Journal of the East African Swahili Committee,* XXVIII (1958).
————. "East African Coin Finds and Their Historical Significance," *Journal of African History,* I (1960).
————. "Historiography of the East African Coast," *Tanganyika Notes and Records,* LV (1960).
GOLDS, J. M. "African Urbanisation in Kenya," *Journal of African Administration,* XIII (1959).
HINSLEY, A. "The Romance of Mombasa from the XVth to the XVIIth Centuries," *East African Annual* (1932–33).
JOHNSTONE, H. B. "Notes on the Customs of the Tribes Inhabiting the Mombasa Subdistrict," *Journal of the Royal African Institute* (1902).
KIRKMAN, J. S. "Historical Archaeology in Kenya, 1948–1956," *Antiquaries' Journal,* XXXVII (1957).
————. "The Culture of the Kenya Coast in the Later Middle Ages," *South African Archaeological Bulletin,* II (1956).
MATHEW, G. "The Culture of the East African Coast in the 17th and 18th Centuries," *Man,* LVI (1956).
NOBLE, D. S. "The Coastal Dhow Trade of Kenya" *Geographical Journal,* CXXIX (1963).
OMINDE, H. "Population Movements to the Main Urban Areas of Kenya," *Cahier Etudes Africaines,* XX (1965).

O'NEILL, H. L. "The Ancient Civilisation, Trade and Commerce of Eastern Africa," *Scottish Geographical Magazine* (1886).

PRINS, A. H. J. "On Swahili Historiography," *Journal of the East African Swahili Commission,* XXVIII (1958).

SILBERMAN, L. "The Social Survey of the Old Town of Mombasa," *Journal of African Administration,* II (1950).

VAN DONGEN, I. S. "Mombasa in the Land and Sea Exchanges of East Africa," *Erdkunde,* XVII (July, 1963), 16–38.

VILLIERS, A. "Some Aspects of the Arab Dhow Trade," *Middle East Journal,* XIII (1946).

WAINWRIGHT, G. A. "Early Foreign Trade in East Africa," *Man,* XLVII (1947).

WILSON, G. M. "Mombasa—A Modern Colonial Municipality," in A. SOUTHALL (ed.), *Social Change in Modern Africa.* London, 1961.

INDEX